Little Big World

sightline books

The Iowa Series in Literary Nonfiction

Patricia Hampl & Carl H. Klaus, series editors

Jeffrey Hammond
Little Big World

Collecting Louis Marx
and the American Fifties

For Evelyn —
With best wishes and
gratitude for your support
over the years.

— JH

University of Iowa Press   Iowa City

University of Iowa Press, Iowa City 52242
Copyright © 2010 by Jeffrey Hammond
www.uiowapress.org
Printed in the United States of America
Text design by Richard Hendel

The University of Iowa Press is a member of
Green Press Initiative and is committed to
preserving natural resources.

Printed on acid-free paper

Library of Congress Cataloging-in-Publication Data
     Little big world: collecting Louis Marx and the
American fifties / Jeffrey Hammond.
          p.   cm.—(Sightline books: the Iowa series in
literary nonfiction)
     ISBN-13: 978-1-58729-910-0 (cloth)
     ISBN-10: 1-58729-910-0 (cloth)
     ISBN-13: 978-1-58729-943-8 (e-book)
     ISBN-10: 1-58729-943-7 (e-book)
     1. Toys—United States—Anecdotes.   2. Toys—
Collectors and collecting—United States.   3. Louis
Marx & Co.—History.   4. Hammond, Jeffrey—
Childhood and youth.   5. Middle West—Social life
and customs—20th century.   I. Title.
     TS2301.T7H29 2010
     688.7'2097309045—dc22   2010006145

FOR RAVISHING DALE,

QUIZZICAL AL,

AND SIMON THE ZEALOT

Contents

Preface and Acknowledgments

I never made a conscious decision to become a collector, let alone a collector of old toys. The impulse ambushed me four years ago while I was working on a longstanding scholarly project: a study of the Gospel of Mark as an ancient cultic text. Although the topic fascinated me, a mysterious lack of energy and concentration was slowing my progress. When I was younger, I could spend whole days doing this kind of work; now, all kinds of pesky distractions kept popping up. One of those distractions was looking at pictures of old toys on eBay—and like any other shirker, I found a way to justify it. Why shouldn't a middle-aged English professor take a break, now and then, by gazing at cherished objects from his childhood? "Now and then" gradually turned into hours at a time, until one day I bought a small group of toy dinosaurs—and I was hooked. Because I loved playing with these figures as a child, nostalgia seemed an obvious motive: isn't the middle-aged man who wants to get his old toys back a cliché of modern times? Things quickly moved beyond nostalgia, however, when I found myself bidding on playset figures that I never owned or even saw before.

I had no interest in acquiring complete playsets; I just wanted the figures. These tiny people and animals were working some sort of spell on me, but I didn't know why. All I knew, as dozens and then hundreds of army men, knights, dollhouse families, firemen, cowboys, Indians, jungle animals, and horses paraded into the house, was that I couldn't get enough of them. It was perfectly clear that collecting old toys had become a way to avoid working on my project. Something else, however, was not so clear: out of all the toys that I might have collected, why had I become fixated on playset figures?

This book, the outgrowth of my attempt to answer that haunting question, is the biography of a collection, but also—inevitably—the autobiography of a collector. The figures that captivated me were included in the quintessential boys' toy of the late fifties and early sixties: the themed playset as developed and sold most successfully by the Louis Marx toy company. The playset offered a miniature version of a particular time and place, whether real or fictive. A setting or backdrop—usually a building to be assembled from sheets of lithographed tin—came with a host of plastic figures and accessories with which a child could act out stories related to the playset's theme. Of the dozens that Marx produced, the most popular included a prehistoric era set, a Civil War set, a Fort Apache set, the Roy Rogers Ranch, the Happi-Time Farm, and several World War II sets.

History might explain something of playsets' appeal. The ancient Egyptians, who believed that the pleasures of this life would continue in the next, routinely placed small human figures in tombs to perform work for the deceased. For funerary objects, these figures are surprisingly unspooky: little boatmen, bakers, hunters, dancers, and guards are merely doing what servants ordinarily did. A miniature version of the deceased was also provided: the mummiform *ushabti*, which would serve as a stand-in if the corpse were ever stolen or destroyed. *Ushabti* figures reflected a buoyantly practical view of the afterlife: what good would eternal pleasures be without a body to enjoy them?

When I saw pictures of these Egyptian figures as a child, I fantasized about playing with them. In so doing, I reimagined them as toys, a common practice whenever industrialized Westerners ponder the artifacts of traditional societies. Given our post-Enlightenment faith in reason, we think it quaint that the "primitive" mind could invest material objects with such life and power. We read *Moby Dick* and smile at Queequeg's "little god," judging his beliefs childlike next to Ahab's more "advanced" theology, with its contending abstractions of good and evil.

Today we call the modern equivalents of Queequeg's little god "dolls" or "action figures," and we restrict their magic to children. Seen historically, this restriction is unusual. In most times and places, miniature representations of people have possessed enormous, even magical appeal. Paleolithic figurines of indeterminate purpose have turned up all over the world; the most famous of these, the Venus of Willendorf, is nicely scaled for a largish dollhouse. Small statues of bald, reed-skirted men with preternaturally large eyes are common relics of ancient Sumer, in the Tigris-Euphrates flatlands. Canaanite figures found at Ugarit typify the cult statues, many small enough for use on home altars, which were popular in all ancient New Eastern and Mediterranean cultures. Little artificial people also turn up in the New World, as witnessed by the kachina dolls of the American Southwest.

Nowadays we deem such objects acceptable as children's toys, but feel vaguely threatened whenever they assert their bold presences to adults. Rod Serling captured this fear in a famous *Twilight Zone* episode in which a ventriloquist's dummy comes aggressively to life, a fear revisited in the figure of Chucky, the malevolent movie-dummy. The disturbing aura of artificial people goes back at least to the Pygmalion story recounted in Ovid's *Metamorphoses*. There, a statue of a woman comes to life with unsettling results; only the sculptor's hasty prayer to Venus saves the day. Dark rumors that the medieval wizard Albertus Magnus constructed a mechanical talking head developed into our mad-scientist stories; indeed, Frankenstein's monster still gives us goose bumps. Toymakers like Signore Geppetto can go mad, too. Not only was Pinocchio mildly creepy, but he was a liar to boot.

Living dolls frighten us not just because they are alive, but because they are small. Our fear of miniature people runs back through Gulliver's Lilliputians and Ireland's leprechauns to the homunculus, the malevolent "little man" of medieval lore. These little people may be cute, sort of—but you don't want to cross them: the pixies of folk tradition were rarely benign. The Age of Reason did not stamp out our uneasy fascination with small quasi-humans: nineteenth-century positivism found its irrational inversion in the fairy craze that swept Victorian England. But what about modern times? Don't the ballet *The Nutcracker*, the book *The Velveteen Rabbit*, and the movies *Small Soldiers* and *Toy Story* reflect ongoing attempts to domesticate a deep-seated fear that if we don't keep an eye on these little figures, they might come to life?

To fear something is, of course, to concede its possibility. This is why the Hebrew Bible warned against all such "dolls" and their powers. Jealous of those Canaanite statuettes, Yahweh prohibited the worship of "graven images" of divine things, including himself. In ancient Jewish tradition, to attribute life—let alone divinity—to an idol like Aaron's golden calf was madness, a belief that was later embraced by devout Muslims. Early Christians agreed: given the ubiquity of cult figures in ancient times, Saint Paul's message to the Athenians about a "God unknown" was, most immediately, a message about a god unseen—a god without an action figure. But Christianity could not resist the universal human impulse to give form to the unseen. An elaborate iconography that began on catacomb walls led to visual depictions even of the all-powerful Creator, the Pantocrator who stares down sternly from the walls and ceilings of basilicas and cathedrals.

As Pygmalion and Dr. Frankenstein both learned, to create an artificial person is an act of unforgivable pride—an arrogant grasping at divine power. What the Western aniconic tradition leaves unstated, however, is the nagging suspicion that artificial people are forbidden because they have powers of their own. Ask any child who loves a doll or an action figure: little artificial people can evoke an almost irresistible sense of animation and personality.

I can attest that the same holds true for artificial people who are even smaller than cult statues, dolls, and action figures: the two- to three-inch figures that came with the playsets that were so popular when I was little. Injection-molded in a variety of cheap plastics, playset figures were, in essence, dolls for little boys. Although playing with them fostered some of the lessons in empathy that playing with dolls traditionally brings, they also fed baser instincts. Every boy of my generation knew the thrill of playset violence: tiny cowboys and Indians fighting over territory and all-out wars between armies of toy soldiers. I also remember quieter moments, however, in which these figures seemed to be playing with *me*. At such moments I was mesmerized by them, and in decidedly unbiblical ways. It's difficult to shake my memory of their power as I gaze at the crowd of little people and animals arranged on my desktop. I can't help seeing these figures as sentient beings who are trying to tell me something that I need to hear, right now.

This book grew out of an essay that appeared in *Small Comforts: Essays at Middle Age* (Kent State University Press, 2008); I remain grateful to Will Underwood, director of the Press, and Joanna Craig, former acquisitions editor, for their support and encouragement. I also wish to thank Larry Vote, provost of St. Mary's College of Maryland, for granting a sabbatical that allowed me to start writing this book, and the Reeves family—Donna, Brad, and Steve—for their generous and ongoing support. A number of friends and colleagues responded helpfully to drafts and shared their expertise on a variety of topics: in particular, Thomas Botzman on plastics, Elizabeth Charlebois on theology, and Jennifer Cognard-Black on play theory and material culture. The manuscript also benefited enormously from Jennifer's discerning eye and ear as a fiction writer and essayist. I also wish to thank Joseph Parsons, Charlotte Wright, and Holly Carver of the University of Iowa Press; Carl Klaus, editor of the Sightline Series; copyeditor Lisa Raffensperger; and an anonymous reviewer for their excellent advice as the book approached final form. My biggest debt is to Norma Tilden of Georgetown University, who graciously put up with these old toys and helped me see why they were worth writing about.

Little Big World

Faces I Remember

W hen I was seven and first encountered Dale Evans as she smiled and stepped forward, hat in hand, I was transfixed. Sixty millimeters tall in rubbery white vinyl and resplendent in her fringed, star-studded western outfit, she was perfect: a free-standing, self-sufficient cowgirl who looked ready for anything. I routinely carried her around in my pocket, pulling her out during quiet times to peer at her face and wonder what she was thinking.

It's over a half-century later, and I'm peering into that face again. My childhood Dale Evans—it now feels right to call her Ravishing Dale—disappeared long ago in the way in which outgrown toys always disappear: that is to say, I don't know what became of her. Although the mint figure that I recently bought on eBay is smaller than I remember and her smile now seems disturbingly aggressive, she still holds considerable appeal. How could she not, when I once loved her more than I loved her real-life counterpart?

A matching Roy Rogers, hands resting on his gun belt as he gazes into the middle distance with a dimpled, inscrutable grin, is here, too—another eBay purchase. Although I can still visualize the real Roy Rogers, happy-faced and squinty-eyed, it is his 60-millimeter counterpart that comes to mind whenever I hear the name. This makes sense, given that I saw the TV adventures of Roy Rogers and Dale Evans only during the last year of the show's run, and then only sporadically because television hurt my eyes and I found it hard to sit still for the half-hour program. Their vinyl avatars, however, were with me constantly: I remember these broad, coarse faces more vividly than the faces of most of my playmates and schoolteachers.

Both figures came with the Western Town playset produced by the

Louis Marx toy company. I received one of these playsets, its "Mineral City" version, for Christmas of 1957. Gazing at Roy and Dale now reminds me of what I felt when I gazed at them then: an inexplicable tranquility, a daydreamlike sense of being timeless and placeless. I wouldn't call this feeling "reflective" or "meditative": those words are too somber and purposeful. It's more a sense that purpose is melting away altogether. A middle-aged man who was raised Methodist but is currently not much of anything will also hesitate to use the word "spiritual" to describe his response to these figures, then or now. And yet, Ravishing Dale and Standing Roy—to distinguish him from Sitting Roy, a laughing jokester who also came with the set—seem to exert a minor-league version of the mesmerizing impact that religious icons have always had on believers. Faces like these are objects transparent to a deeper reality: they are half human and half something else.

Around 150 playset figures made of rubberized vinyl or soft plastic, most between 2½ and 3 inches tall, are standing on my desk to the right of my keyboard. Most are Marx figures, but others were made by the Auburn Rubber Company of Auburn, Indiana; Tim-Mee Toys of Aurora, Illinois; Thomas Toys of Newark; the Multiple Products Corporation; Ideal; Lido; Ohio Art; and four European manufacturers: Atlantic of Italy, Britains of England, and Jecsan and Reamsa of Spain.

Although a few recasts are scattered here and there, most of these toys are originals—"vintage," as the eBay listings like to say. There are cowboys, Indians, soldiers, sailors, construction workers, 1950s celebrities, ancient Romans, ancient Egyptians, American presidents, farmers, bathing beauties, cops, firefighters, knights, and pioneers. Several animals—four horses, an elephant, a dinosaur, a gorilla, a monkey, a dog, and a cat—swell the scene. These are the very best figures that I've acquired over the past four years, the cream of over a thousand that are stored in a nearby bookcase, carefully sorted into plastic bags.

I have arranged the desktop crowd so that they are all gazing at a single spot, where I have placed a Standing Roy atop a barrel as if he's giving a speech. I say *a* Standing Roy because six other Roys are also in attendance, along with six Ravishing Dales, all in the front row and all in rubbery white vinyl. As these figures reveal, the Marx toy company subscribed fully to the fifties mentalité regarding the feminine mystique that Betty Friedan would soon expose: while the Dales are all in a single pose, Roy enjoys three times her mobility. In addition to the Standing Roy who addresses the crowd and the Sitting Roy who looks as if he's slapping his knee at an off-color joke, a third Roy—I call him Aggressive Roy—steps forward with a wary expression and a drawn gun. As a child I did not find the existence of two Roys confusing, though I was probably lucky not to own this third figure. Three Roys might have thrown me, as if I were being prematurely confronted with the paradox of the Trinity.

The presence of multiple Roys and Dales brings no discomfort now, only an atavistic satisfaction that I hope reflects something other than mere greed. As I gaze at the thirteen Roys and Dales before me, it occurs to me that the only thing better would be gazing at twenty-six of them. Here, in vintage vinyl, is tangible proof of the profound appeal of visual rhythm and spatial repetition. This same appeal generated another embodiment of the aesthetics of excess that held sway when I was growing up: the Rockettes. If one dancer doing high kicks is diverting, thirty will be spectacular.

The potential monotony of multiple playset people in identical poses will not disturb a collector, for whom no two figures are ever the same. All collectors develop this hyper-discernment, this eye for fine distinctions lost on outsiders. Of the three Standing Roys, for instance, the head of one bends down at a slightly greater angle, which makes him—it should be clear by now that an object this appealing cannot be an "it"—appear broodier than the others. The Dales exhibit similar variations within sameness: one leans forward more than her sisters; another, scarcely played with, gleams like polished ivory; a third is slightly grayed with play-grime that sharpens her features. Like an appraiser of Stickley furniture or Hockney prints, I see things that others cannot. Each figure is unique to me—a source of pride and embarrassment, in roughly equal measure.

Don't we always love first, and only later shape ethical structures to justify it? During the past four years I have unwittingly developed a moral framework that allows me to keep mailing checks to strangers and receiving dozens of little boxes in return. I've even convinced myself that opening these boxes is an act of altruism which allows these figures, secure in the safety of numbers, to relax a little.

A 60-millimeter Dale who has managed to stay in the world for fifty years is a brave but vulnerable thing—and even though a smiling cowgirl can get the blues, a half-dozen of them will never feel alone. Acquired at considerable cost and effort, my Dales can also feel reasonably safe from the hell of all playset figures: the landfill. Seven Roys might similarly be expected to handle what one Roy, unsteady on slightly warped feet, cannot. What's more, a vinyl cowboy in three poses can exorcize landfill terrors in more than one way: he can be wary and reflective and goofy all at once.

A law of lost-things probabilities—the mathematical equivalent to praying to Saint Anthony—is at work here. A middle-aged man who has collected thirteen Roys and Dales has upped the odds that among them are *his* Roys and Dale, the very figures that he once loved but left behind in a cigar box, probably to be sold (this is a guess) in a yard sale that his parents held when he was off at college. "Do you want us to keep any of your old toys?" I clearly recall my mother asking this question in a phone conversation, though not my exact reply. It must have been something like: "Of course not! I'm a grown-up; why would you even ask me such a thing?"

An actual grown-up—that is, someone familiar with the sobering effects of time—would have answered quite differently. The whiny urgency of "Don't sell Roy and Dale!" would reflect the grown-up's knowledge that the real-life counterparts of these figures once brought many children a lot of happiness but are now dead, separated not only from each other but from all creature comforts. All flesh is grass, but rubberized vinyl is forever—or can be, if it isn't swept away by a mother's rage for order and a son's defensiveness. These tiny survivors on my desk both confirm and defy the fact that, sooner or later, all real cowboys and cowgirls eventually head on down the trail. My Marx Western Town, fresh out of the box, was already exposing the strongest verb in the grammar of living things: I die, you die, he/she/it dies, we die, you-all die, they die.

Or not. Even a former boy-Methodist with a melancholy streak will affirm that old toys can effect tiny resurrections. Time indeed "marches on," as the cliché goes, but time can also loop back onto itself in weird epicycles. What is a vivid memory, after all, but a temporary reversal of time's rush? And what is a childhood toy if not a vivid memory in tangible form, a material link with the former self who once played with it?

Middle-aged nostalgia might be raising its gauzy head here, but if nostalgia consists of a yearning for lost times and places, I am innocent. I have no desire to return to my boyhood, which I remember as long stretches of purposeless reverie punctuated by occasional but intense moments of anxiety. No *Lone Ranger* announcer is calling me back to "those thrilling days of yesteryear," because I actually *remember* those days—and truth be told, they weren't all that thrilling. Yes, I want to get my old toys back, just like countless other midlife guys with eBay names like "YazForever," "ElvisLives," and "Boomer1950," but I want them with me as I am now. I want to incorporate them into the chastened consciousness of a grown-up for whom time is indeed marching on, and with alarming speed. There's a fantasy of escape here, but with a difference that I hope saves me from being a walking cliché: I want to stop time, or at least slow it down a little, not by returning to the past but by giving time some flexibility in my here and now. To see and handle a toy from one's childhood is to oppose the unforgiving rigidities of chronology—to achieve an illusion of agency in the face of time's inevitable flow. I didn't know that I wanted to do this, or even that it was doable, until these 60-millimeter people started parading back into my life.

If a daydream of stepping out of time's relentless flow, however briefly, sounds silly, at least I'm not alone: the ancients dreamt it, too. In Hellenistic Greek, two words were commonly used for time: *chronos* and *kairos*. As the word "chronology" suggests, *chronos* denoted time in a neutral, absolute sense: time in and of itself, ongoing and measurable as "the days of our lives," in fifties TV parlance. By contrast, *kairos* denoted a time in which something could happen: a fitting or opportune time, a "season." *Kairos* was time *for* something— that is, time plus significance. The distinction between absolute time and time-with-significance took many forms. Farmers linked *kairos* to the proper times for planting and harvesting. For rhetoricians, *kairos* referred to the right time or occasion for a speech. In religious discourse, especially among early Christians, *kairos* came to denote times of unusual spiritual energy: moments in which the human and divine realms intersected. To experience a *kairos* moment was to break into sacred time—and for the ancients, sacred time was not "no time" but a God's-eye embrace of *all* time.

This old distinction seems useful for describing what Roy and Dale have reanimated in me. It is also consistent with what fifties playsets were all about: achieving a godlike sense of all time collapsing into the sacred here and now of play. What was a playset if not an assemblage of tin and plastic parts that a child could arrange and rearrange with absolute power? A small person in control of even smaller people, I could look down, quite literally, on Roy, Dale, and the cowboys that came with them. They always did my bidding.

I vividly remember setting up the Western Town street front, complete with hotel and bank, and arranging these figures into endless vignettes and narratives of my own making. These escapes into the imaginary time and place of Mineral City took me out of Cold War Ohio just as surely as a similar daydream had taken the real Roy Rogers out of Depression-era Ohio a quarter-century earlier. What's more, to play with vinyl Roy was to enter the same all-time realm that flesh-and-blood Roy entered when he began his career in show business: an imagined West in which past, present, and future were all telescoped into a single, happy-trails moment. If ancient *kairos* was time for something, playset *kairos* defined that something as *nothing*, as an escape from immediate time, place, and purpose into another realm altogether. While this all-time zone might seem unattainable now, something left behind with a child's imaginings, the figures on my desk are proving otherwise. Simply looking at them is generating some time-bending epiphanies.

When I opened that big package on Christmas morning of 1957 and confronted vinyl Roy and vinyl Dale, freshly popped from their molds at the Marx factory in Glen Dale, West Virginia, the flesh-and-blood Roy was in his mid-forties. He had already been a Hollywood star for over a decade when he made the move from film and radio to the new medium of television in 1951. It would be twenty years before he would acquire his primary significance for later generations by lending his name to a fast-food franchise that needed a famous cowboy to sell roast beef—and who better than the King of the Cowboys?

The figures on my desk predate the use of a showbiz legend to sell fast food. Indeed, they predate fast food itself. These Roys and Dales came into the world when long-distance calls were still being placed from Los Angeles by a hardworking TV star to friends and family back home in southern Ohio—calls that were still being answered with "Lenny! How *are* you?" I can't imagine Leonard Slye admitting in these conversations that he was ever tired or sad. He had refashioned himself into Roy Rogers, King of the Cowboys: how could someone who was so clearly living the American Dream feel blue amid the upbeat bustle of show business, let alone complain about it?

Staring at this desktop, I imagine the trio of 60-millimeter Roys as fiercely present stand-ins for the long-gone Leonard Slye: they usurp his conversation and bring it into my hearing. It is Sitting Roy, grinning like a fool, who is doing most of the talking, entertaining the home folks with funny stories about Hollywood and proving, he hopes, that he hasn't changed all that much. Aggressive Roy, a stoic in fringes, grabs the phone to assure his hearer—I'm imagining an old friend from school, before Lenny dropped out to go to work—that everything is fine, just fine, really. Lenny doesn't mention that they're already two days behind in this week's shooting schedule, or that his agent has overbooked this month's personal appearances. As the conversation draws to a close, it is Standing Roy, he of the noncommittal grin, who wonders what it all means. Things have gotten a little crazy out here in California—and naturally, Lenny would always think of California as "out here."

A no-longer-young TV cowboy spending twelve-hour days on a sound stage might have something in common with a toy collector who is fifteen years older than the tired man who is making that call. Both might be noticing increasing habit of weariness, a bit less pep in the old step. The showbiz cowboy may even have felt as boxed, sold, and played with as his 60-millimeter counterparts on my desk. If so, he might have welcomed a toy cowboy of his own—perhaps a rubber Hoot Gibson, had one existed—to dispel his own bent-head broodiness.

It's not difficult to imagine that on the very day in which the Standing Roy who addresses his playset peers was leaving the Glen Dale plant on the banks of the Ohio River, his flesh-and-blood prototype was telling his old pal that he hopes to visit soon but hot damn this television is sure enough a crank-'em-out deal; no rest for the wicked, dontcha know?

As he uttered these words, Roy might have been remembering the broad, brown stillness of that same river. Some three hundred miles downstream from the Marx plant, the Ohio flowed three blocks away from the 2nd Street tenement in Cincinnati where Leonard Franklin Slye was born—the site, sixty years later, of the Reds' Riverfront Stadium. Lenny would never forget that river: the Slye family moved upstream to Portsmouth when he was still a baby and lived on a houseboat until he was seven. Then they moved to a farm in Duck Run, near Lucasville, where Lenny learned to handle horses. His father Andy must have intuited what the coming Depression would teach millions of others: if you've got land and water, you won't starve. Being smart, of course, doesn't mean that things always work out. When Lenny was seventeen, the family gave up their dream of living off the land and moved back to the big town, where he took a job with his father in a shoe factory. It wouldn't be long before Los Angeles would show the Slyes what a big town really was. In 1930 the family left Cincinnati for southern California, where Lenny and his father drove trucks and worked in construction and in the fields, following the harvests and living in the migratory workers' camps.

At the time there was a rich fantasy world—a cheerful alternative to the dour realities of failed banks and big-city breadlines—growing by leaps and bounds in the Los Angeles suburb of Hollywood. Popular entertainment was becoming an indispensable distraction for the struggling nation, and with western music booming right along with the movies, it didn't take Lenny long to see that a young, good-looking guy who could sing in a sweet but non-sissy manner could find softer work than driving a truck or picking tomatoes. Lenny and his cousin Stanley tried to break into this fantasy world by forming, with little success, an act called the Slye Brothers—exactly the sort of no-nonsense name that a pair of practical Buckeyes would choose for themselves.

Lenny had gotten considerably more poetic by 1934, when he founded another singing group and called it the Sons of the Pioneers. The Sons enjoyed far greater success than the "brother" act, and within a year Lenny landed a bit part in a movie. After performing competently in a series of supporting roles, he got his big break in 1938, when he was rechristened Roy Rogers, supposedly after his Duck Run dentist, and promoted as a competitor to the original singing cowboy, Gene Autry. Almost immediately, he became a box-office star.

Roy's success as an actor makes it easy to forget that he was primarily a singer. He was also precisely what his vinyl avatars are warning me *not* to be: a confirmed nostalgist. Wasn't Roy's new identity inextricably rooted in loss? The name of his vocal group contained a latent acknowledgment that the real Old West, as opposed to the imaginary place where money could be made, had already gone to the landfill with the real pioneers: now only their "sons" remained. This lost West would become Roy Rogers's proto-playset nowhere and no-time: a showbiz cowboy's indigenous turf, grounded in its own absence.

Although my Mineral City playset encouraged an unabashed celebration of this mythical West, its very name revealed the dissolution of the realm that it celebrated. Despite the horses and cattle and fences, it was mining, not ranching, that drove its tin-litho economy. That the Marx company produced a variant set under the name Silver City underscored the absent West with even greater clarity. In the mythical history of humankind recorded in Ovid's *Metamorphoses*, four ages trace a sad devolution from virtue to vice, with mining the bowels of Mother Earth a hallmark of the final and most hellish age. Mineral City, it seems, had already suffered a precipitous fall from playset Eden. Every postlapsarian tree demands a snake: didn't the set come with a bank and a bank robber?

As Saint Paul confirmed in 1 Timothy, *cupiditas radix malorum*: desire is the root of all evil. Of course, if you were young in the thirties, what you most desired was money. Roy must have heard that biblical warning about having two masters, God and Mammon, but times are pretty damned hard, dontcha know? Though no theologian, Roy could attest that Mammon took a frightful toll. As I visualize the forty-six-year-old cowboy shuffling back to the set—Hot damn, these boots pinch!—to memorize some inane dialogue for his next scene, I can't resist injecting a melodramatic note that harmonizes with my own middle-age keening, and perhaps also with his: Roy is entertaining vague fantasies of oblivion. I don't see him thinking these thoughts in a morbid or self-pitying way unworthy of the King of the Cowboys, but in the quiet, familiar manner of a bone-tired teenager who has just ended his shift at an Ohio shoe factory and knows about Hollywood only from magazines at the drugstore.

This ex-teenager, now burdened with the playwear of middle age, walks back onto the set and directs a weary nod toward sidekick Pat Brady, another transplanted Ohioan who is living the Hollywood dream. While Roy glances at the leftover sandwiches on the catering table, Lenny is remembering the sauerbraten and red cabbage that he and the old gang used to enjoy back in Cincinnati. Or perhaps he's thinking of the old house in Duck Run. A half-century later, the Cleveland *Plain Dealer* would report that the current owners of the house tried to sell it for $70,000, but got no takers. It's a good thing that Roy isn't psychic. He doesn't need a premonition of this non-event to sharpen his awareness that for TV cowboys, as for everyone else, *sic transit gloria mundi*. Although he hasn't told his agent yet, he has already decided that this will be the show's final season.

Pat Brady, born in Toledo in 1914 but reborn, like his boss, as a gen-u-wine westerner, is also standing in the crowd on my desk. Unlike the Roys and Dales, Pat has been molded in the later soft plastic. His face is a little chewed up, and with one hand on his hat and his mouth open, he looks perpetually surprised. The flesh-and-blood Pat Brady died in 1972 when he was only fifty-seven, three years younger than I am now. Here on my desk, though, he's still sneaking peeks at Ravishing Dale. This is not lust, exactly; it's just that like everyone else, he's crazy about her. Dale is Pat's favorite figure, too.

Pat Brady surely knew, as his plastic counterpart seems to know, that with real people and toy people alike, love resides in the details. Lucille Wood Smith, soon renamed Frances Octavia Smith, was born in a small Texas town in 1912, a year later than Roy. Lucille/Frances picked up her third name—the one that stuck—during her rise as a swing and big-band singer, another refugee from the real world to the make-believe world of show business. Unlike the two transplanted Buckeyes with whom she became a star, Dale Evans was a genuine westerner, though as a jazzy vocalist her sensibilities were more country hipster—I'm imagining an early Patsy Cline—than rustic cowgirl. Around the time when she and Roy were first cast together in a movie in 1945, Roy's second wife Arline died in childbirth and Dale divorced her third husband. Once Roy and Dale got married, the turmoil that had marked their personal lives was finally at an end. They would be together for over fifty years, until Roy's death in 1998 at the age of eighty-seven. Dale would follow three years later, when she was eighty-nine.

Back on the set, Dale is ignoring Pat Brady's moon-calf looks in that cheerful manner of women who know how attractive they are but don't want to hurt anyone's feelings. Although she would surely disapprove of my calling her vinyl counterpart Ravishing Dale, she wouldn't make a big deal over it: she was too busy to waste time correcting every male indiscretion that she encountered. A talented and prolific songwriter, Dale wrote around 300 songs, including that Sunday-school staple of my childhood: "Yes, Jesus Loves Me." Her most famous secular song, "Happy Trails," became her and Roy's theme. Given what the pair had gone through, the song's hopeful lyrics—"Happy trails to you until we meet again"—seem more poignant than serene, an expression of hope rather than attainment. Dale's trail had been anything but happy, but it made her as tough and resilient as her rubbery avatars on my desk. A year after eloping at fourteen, she gave birth to a son whom agents and promoters, not wanting to dampen her romantic appeal, passed off as her little brother. The show must go on.

The young mother who was singing her way through the Great Depression had no way of knowing that she was beginning her own transformation. Within ten years, this sexy, full-lipped, swing-music gal would become a moral compass for America, an icon of right living for the forties, fifties, and beyond. I see Dale's story as a saddle-and-reins *imitatio Christi*. As with the Jesus to whom she drew closer as she aged, it was suffering, not success, that effected her sanctification. After her only child with Roy, Robin Elizabeth, died before her second birthday from complications arising from Down Syndrome, Dale wrote a best-selling inspirational book called *Angel Unaware*; its 1953 edition featured an introduction by Norman Vincent Peale. For the rest of her life she remained a major presence in devotional music and religious television. She and Roy also became lifelong advocates for the welfare of children as well as active promoters of adoption. Personal taste aside, Dale's corresponding musical evolution—from swing through country to gospel—seems not just hard-won but heartfelt, the reflection of an authentic personal journey. I've taken to reading the fierce smile on her 60-millimeter counterpart as a badge of courage, no doubt bright red with fifties lipstick if she had been factory painted. Yes, Jesus loved her. But then again, who wouldn't?

Roy and Dale's TV show ended in 1957, which put me at the tail end of their original audience, although millions of later kids would know them through reruns. When I was playing with vinyl Roy and vinyl Dale, I had no idea that the King of the Cowboys and the Queen of the West had led such complicated lives—that they were on their third and fourth marriages and had faced the sort of tragedy that children cannot imagine. Nor would I have guessed that Roy's Duck Run home, a small bungalow with dormer windows, was nearly identical to the house in which I was playing with his vinyl avatars. At the time, I would have denied that Roy and Dale ever occupied such mundane space. To me they lived in a perpetual sunny day with their horses, Trigger and Buttermilk, their faithful dog Bullet, and that open-mouthed sidekick Pat Brady, who was constantly tinkering with his Jeep, Nellybelle. I remember this make-believe realm as a place where nothing changed and everything turned out all right in the end. I could escape to this place whenever I played with their tiny counterparts.

If Roy and Dale gave design approval to their playset versions, they must have been utterly devoid of vanity. The three faces of Roy now strike me as thick and blocky: Sitting Roy has some personality, albeit on the goofy side, but Standing Roy looks stupid and Aggressive Roy looks brutal. Dale's face, big and bovine and grinning a little too broadly, is alarmingly large for her body. Perhaps flesh-and-blood Roy figured that kids would pay little attention to his playset faces; if so, I'm living proof that he was wrong about that. Perhaps flesh-and-blood Dale felt that the spectacular outfit and hairdo of her vinyl version compensated for its manic expression. Or maybe—and this is the conclusion that satisfies me the most—they had suffered their way beyond such vanities. Although no other showbiz couple, with the possible exception of Lucy and Desi, had achieved greater popular success, the most obvious facts aren't always the most telling ones. Robin Elizabeth died around the time that these figures were first produced: is there any wonder that Dale's smile looks forced, or that Roy is beside himself three times over?

When viewed free from the expectations of realism, however,

these unflattering faces take on an unexpected appropriateness. Standing Roy and Ravishing Dale were not replicas but toys, objects designed to stimulate a child's imagination. Their faces inhabited a kind of no-man's-land between representation and symbol, between casual attempts to reproduce the couple's actual features and a stronger impulse to give them the idealized look of the archetypal cowboy and cowgirl.

Given how these faces assert a twofold reality—the living Roy and Dale, but also a mythical West that transcended them—it does not seem an overstatement to call these figures iconic, to see them as pop-culture equivalents to far older faces that also represented something beyond themselves. Medieval portraits of the saints were unrealistic, too. Why submit to optical realism when the whole point was to get beyond what the eye can see? The playset figure and the religious icon share an underlying purpose: each is less a thing in itself than a vehicle of its own imaginative transcendence. As a medieval worshiper you weren't supposed to glance at an icon of Saint Luke, luminous and otherworldly in its gilt flatness, say "Yep, there's Saint Luke," and look away. You were supposed to stare at that face until your purpose-drained gaze broke through to another reality to which the painted image was only a door. Vinyl Roy and vinyl Dale were like that. Until they came to life as actors in a child's imagined stories, they remained inert lumps of processed petroleum. They could not be encountered passively; you were supposed to *play* with them. And when you did, you traded your own time and place for an eternal realm that has always haunted the American mind: the playset-like *kairos* of the perpetually wild and endlessly reimagined West.

That such momentless moments might be accessible even in these latter days seems clear from the fact that everyone standing in this neat row on my desk is simultaneously long gone and together again, boldly present in an artifactual quasi-permanence. These figures were once played with by children who are gone: if not dead, then gone in the sense that they are no longer children—and they, too, are inseparable from the history of these toys, from their provenance. This latter term might seem more fitting for a Matisse cutout than for little vinyl people, but no matter. I imagine these absent children forming a caravan of ghosts, including my own boy-ghost, stretching from the fifties to this moment and this desktop, a chain of consciousness rendered incarnate in the 60-millimeter community that stands before me.

It stands there, at least, for now—an afterthought suggestive of the fact that seemingly purposeless play is never as purposeless as it seems. These playset people are reminding me of real people who are no longer here. Someday, of course, these figures and I won't be here either. My Roys and Dales will go to another collector, an actual child, or a landfill, depending on how their luck holds. As for me, I will follow flesh-and-blood Roy, flesh-and-blood Dale, and the children who played with their vinyl avatars into whatever Happy Trail awaits all once and future cowpokes.

But that's the strange thing about icons: they make mutability more bearable. As I gaze into these faces, the rush of time seems less disturbing than it would be if I weren't looking at them. A half-remembered sense that everything will turn out all right in the end surely accounts for my deep satisfaction in seeing so many Roys and Dales together, basking in their multiple presences. And basking is definitely in order, because these figures are the lucky ones. All toys, if they don't get broken in their prime, undergo a standard lifecycle: newness, intense play, sporadic play, neglect, storage, and destruction. Outgrown and forgotten, these tiny lumps of rubberized vinyl made it all the way from the Cold War into the twenty-first century: how could they not prompt the startling realization that I've come that far, too? The least I can do is take care of these fellow survivors—to re-animate them, and maybe myself, by playing with them again.

I'm beginning to see why I need these old toys—and especially, why now. Any vintage item from the Eisenhower years, whether in vinyl or flesh and blood, might welcome an opportunity to play with time, however ineffectually, through small acts that a focused imagination cannot help investing with ritual efficacy. Didn't Roy and Dale obey a similar impulse when they sent their beloved Trigger and Bullet to the taxidermist? If a horse and a dog can hang on as museum exhibits for all to see a half-century later, it might not be all that strange to take a little girl from the Marx dollhouse family and place her between my most playworn Dale and my most playworn Roy. Indeed, a sixty-year-old man might deem this small act not just appropriate, but mandatory.

What might Ravishing Dale be thinking about the giant playset figure—that big, jointed doll—who has just placed Robin beside her? Dale is grateful for the gesture, of course, but slightly confused: there's something familiar about the giant's face, though not the wrinkled skin, sagging jowls, and graying hair. He also moves more slowly than she remembers. Didn't there used to be more action? A quicker tempo of play? Clearly, something has changed: although the boy in Dale's memory took little interest in endings, that looming figure now seems obsessed with them—or more accurately, with evading them.

I had a variety of toys as a child: six-shooters, dump trucks, paddleballs, board games. Out of all these once-loved objects, why have playset figures returned to haunt me in late middle age? Roy and Dale, past masters at teaching life lessons through make-believe, seem to suggest an answer. At this moment, Standing Roy's ambiguous grin looks like a philosopher's response to the mad rush of time; Dale's broad smile betrays an even deeper acceptance of endings and rumors of endings. Even after all these years, these two look ready for anything.

A dump truck might generate a memory of filling it with sand, but this memory would only take you back: it would do nothing to move you forward. An old six-shooter might remind you of the cowboy that you once pretended to be, but you haven't been a cowboy for years—not even a pretend one. Unlike these toys, little plastic people seem to look back at you. By confronting you as you are, right here and right now, they demand a current response. Their uncanny assertion of presence draws me into an odd sense of sociability—a feeling that I'm not alone here. Perhaps my seemingly irrational love for these figures has a hard-nosed, practical side after all. Aren't we all forced, at a certain stage of life, to confront the ephemeral nature of all things, including ourselves? What better company for coping with this unsettling notion than a bunch of little people who knew us before our eyes got bad, our joints started aching, and old age began morphing from a vague abstraction into an impending reality?

As eyewitnesses to my "before," these figures might have unusual empathy with my "after." The ever-upbeat Roy and Dale appear eager to help me summon a little bravery—and it seems only fair that I help them, too. Ever the arranger and re-arranger of playset figures, I place a soft plastic Bullet nearby, ears erect and tongue hanging out in a dog's smile, to stand guard over the reincarnated family. Next comes a mint vinyl Trigger, mouth open and eager to take the bit for another ride through a West that was already gone when Roy was training flesh-and-blood Trigger not to get spooked by studio lights or a camera's whir. I position and reposition the little family until everything feels right. Everyone is here, together again.

Once you create a reality, even a make-believe one, you own it. What's more, you had better make the best of it. Though I was born seven months before Robin Elizabeth Rogers, only one of us lived long enough to play with these tiny versions of her parents. By reuniting Robin with her family, if only at 60-millimeter scale, I am rolling time back to a point before either of us realized that every story, whether in vinyl or flesh and blood, comes to an end.

The Prospero of Fifth Avenue

irectly behind the multiple Roys and Dales stands a 60-millimeter Louis Marx, the manufacturer of roughly two-thirds of the playset people congregated on this desktop. Most fifties children, even in our small Ohio town, were familiar with the magical-sounding address of Louis Marx and Company—200 Fifth Avenue, New York 10, New York—along with a marketing slogan phrased in language that was archaic even then: "One of the many Marx toys: have you all of them?" An ongoing legacy of boomer desire began with the fact that having all of them was virtually impossible: in those days the company was making one out of every five toys sold in America. In December of 1955, Louis Marx appeared, cheek to jowl with Santa, on the cover of *Time* magazine as "the Toy King." No one deserved the title more, or offered a clearer example of the American Dream that was so dear to the fifties mindset.

The 60-millimeter Louis Marx is an unusual playset figure, to say the least. Aggressively and poignantly referential, it offers a surreal link between this desktop community and the larger world that its members once represented. Judging from the *Time* cover, I'd say that this tiny, balding impresario, who stares pleasantly into the middle distance with one hand holding a cigar and the other jammed into a rumpled suit pocket, is a very good likeness. The figure—I can't resist calling it the Marx Marx—emulates the style of the U.S. presidents that the company issued in the fifties: gleaming white hard plastic on a square base, with crisp detailing that seems sculpted rather than molded. Although the Marx Marx is a beautiful figure, I would have found it puzzling had I encountered it as a child. "Who's *this* supposed to be?"

The question would have been ironic, because Marx playset figures were central to my childhood. My favorites, in addition to Roy and Dale, were fourteen dinosaurs that I received for Christmas two weeks after that issue of *Time* came out. I also owned about a hundred Marx army men: the 45-millimeter Armed Forces Training Center figures, the 54-millimeter Battleground G.I.s and their opponents, and around twenty 60-millimeter soldiers in various poses. I also spent countless hours playing with the Marx presidents, a Christmas present from 1958 or 1959. My childhood devotion to these toys prompts a twinge of guilt whenever I regard the genial figure standing in the second row of this desktop crowd. Although Louis Marx brought me hours of happiness, I knew nothing about the man except his New York address.

I'm making up for that neglect now. Placing the Marx Marx among his creations grants the figure something of the powerful aura that must have surrounded its flesh-and-blood prototype—a sense of restrained energy beneath placid appearances. Louis Marx stands on this desktop as Prospero to the playset Ariels and Calabans that surround him, his presence conferring real-world validation on all the others. And yet that presence raises a question: why does this figure even exist? Why would the flesh-and-blood Louis Marx make a hard-plastic Louis Marx? What sort of toy was this little man in a suit intended to be?

The answer is simple: the Marx Marx wasn't really a toy at all. By all accounts, the figure was never sold commercially, but served as a tongue-in-cheek promotional item for sales reps to hand out to retailers and other clients. The Marx Marx was a grown-up's bauble, not unlike the even more grown-up "bathing beauties," eight 60-millimeter pinup girls wearing the skimpiest swimsuits that a fifties toy designer could get away with. It's easy to imagine a breezy Marx salesman closing a big deal with Sears or Montgomery Ward and asking the buyer's preference: "What'll it be, Jack? One of these little cuties, or the man himself?"

Thanks to eBay, I don't have to make so difficult a choice. Not only is an original Louis Marx standing here, but purple recasts of the bathing beauties are scattered throughout the desktop crowd. One of them has even charmed her way up to the second row, where she rests an arm on the boss's shoulder and contemplates her image in a mirror. Clearly, this gal knows how to mind the main chance.

So did her maker. Born in Brooklyn in 1896 to German Jewish immigrants, Louis Marx founded the company in 1919 with his brother David, who served as its day-to-day manager. After Louis—he pronounced it "Looee"—bought the rights to Zippo the Climbing Monkey and the Alabama Minstrel Dancer from his former boss, toymaker Ferdinand Strauss, the resulting profits allowed him to buy out the manufacturer whom he had hired to produce these items. Thus began a remarkable string of successes that lasted for over four decades, from the 1928 Yo-Yo, which Marx popularized but did not invent, through the introduction of the ubiquitous and noisy Big Wheel in 1969.

During the Depression Marx acquired factories in Erie and Girard, Pennsylvania, and Glen Dale, West Virginia. The Erie plant was known locally as the "Monkey Works" in honor of Zippo, a reflection of Marx's early success with mechanical and wind-up toys. The Girard plant specialized in trains, while the Glen Dale plant produced cars and other vehicles. The Toy Industry Hall of Fame aptly calls Marx "the Henry Ford of toys": mass-production techniques allowed him to offer, in his words, "more toy for less money." Marx's success rested on low prices, consistent quality—another of his mottos was "Quality is not negotiable"—and his uncanny feel for the market. In the *Time* profile, Marx boasted that he had spent only $312 on advertising for all of 1955, thereby showing an unusual willingness to rely on word of mouth in an era that would come to be known as the golden age of advertising. Like all successful manufacturers, the Marx company gave consumers what they didn't know they wanted until they saw it, and what they saw nearly always fit hand in glove with American popular taste.

The broad, benign face looking out from the old *Time* cover is nicely replicated on the 60-millimeter figure standing before me: both have the open but unreadable expression of a man who is pondering something, not unlike many of his playset figures. But while other photographs reveal a short, portly man who seems uncomfortable being noticed, Louis Marx was hardly a recluse. He lived his American

Dream to the fullest, with Broadway openings, celebrity-studded parties, and frequent dinners at the 21 Club, where he had his own table. The Toy King did well and did good, enjoying a well-deserved reputation as an active and generous philanthropist. He was also fond of socializing with the most famous and powerful people in show business, politics, and especially the military. As Jamie Fenske reports in *Wonderful West Virginia* magazine, "rival toymakers complained that Marx collected generals like a child collects toys." Proud of his service in the army during the First World War, Marx was even prouder of his subsequent rise through the civilian ranks. It's a safe bet that he saw himself as a business-world peer to the Pentagon's top brass: the toy industry's only five-star general.

Several actual generals were godfathers to Marx's children; he was especially close to Eisenhower, who appointed him as an advisor to help rebuild German industry after the war. A number of "commemorative" figures, molded in the same scale, color, and plastic with which Marx rendered himself and the presidents, celebrate the lofty circles in which he ran. Although the presidents were an understandable success in light of postwar American patriotism, the decision to celebrate his military friends in a set of 60-millimeter generals seems more personal than commercial: what was the play appeal of these tiny Omar Bradleys and George Pattons? Other Marx figures that honored power and achievement included the British royal family, a Pope Pius XII, a Cardinal Spellman of New York, a Pinky Lee, and two poses of Jackie Gleason. To be rendered in plastic by Louis Marx was the ultimate confirmation of fifties celebrity.

Part of living the American Dream, of course, is giving your children the luxury of living their own version of it, even if their version is not yours. Among the children of this ultimate capitalist were two seekers whose values ran contrary to their father's. Barbara became a popular speaker and writer on spiritual topics with a decidedly New Age slant, and Patricia became a peace activist whose first date with future husband Daniel Ellsberg of Pentagon Papers fame consisted of attending an antiwar rally.

I can't imagine the old man endorsing either path. Although Barbara Marx Hubbard concedes that most children would envy having the Toy King for a father, she has lamented growing up in a secular household where materialism held sway. In a book called *Conscious*

Evolution, she recalls that her father "told his children that the purpose of life was to win, to make money." As a young girl who sensed something missing, Barbara once asked her father "What religion are we?" His answer was "You are an American. Do your best!"

Though I agree with Barbara's take on materialism, I believe that she is being too hard on her father. It must have taken courage to be an agnostic Jew in the twenties, a time when the Scopes "monkey trial" filled the headlines and aging ballplayer-turned-evangelist Billy Sunday was still packing them in at revivals. With courage comes grace: I imagine Louis Marx making his way through the bare-knuckled world of American industry as gently as he knew how, like his striding trachodon dinosaur with its alert gaze. This grace was appreciated by his employees. A few years ago, the Official Marx Toy Museum in Moundsville, West Virginia, hosted a reunion of former employees from the nearby Glen Dale plant. According to the museum Web site, fingers lost to machinery and sharp-edged sheets of tin did not keep these workers from feeling that they had been part of a "family." Not only were most plant supervisors promoted from within the ranks, but the Glen Dale factory was a union shop in an era when many manufacturers fought tirelessly to keep the unions out. Further evidence for the genial Louis Marx whom I seek comes from a 1954 letter owned by Marx historian Francis Turner, who operates the Moundsville museum. The letter, quoted by Fenske, is the Toy King's personal reply to a woman who had written the company to ask about the availability of firefighter toys. Confirming that a Fire House playset was in production, Marx promised to send her a complimentary unit as soon as it was available.

The boss's ability to laugh at himself is suggested by two other promotional giveaways. The first, a figure of Napoleon with the face of Louis Marx, might indicate low company morale were it not for the simple fact that it exists. Would a truly imperious executive have approved its production? The second is a six-inch Chairman Mao with Louis Marx's face: a blatant visual pun on "Marxism" and the Toy King's fervent embrace of capitalism. These two figures give comic expression to a core ideal of fifties America: it was a society predicated on new and improved identities; a place where you could become whoever you wanted to be. Hadn't the boss done that very thing, first in real life and now in plastic?

The 60-millimeter Louis Marx does not betray the self-image of a narcissist. On the contrary, the figure depicts a middle-aged man who seems, for the moment, less Prospero than Lear: a man bewildered by two independent daughters who cannot see that their father is a seeker, too, a philosopher and cultural anthropologist in tin and plastic. And didn't Marx get rich doing less harm than many others who amassed fortunes during that era? He was sufficiently intelligent and ambitious to have produced toxic chemicals or, during those early Prohibition years, bootleg whiskey. Instead, he made good toys that were cheap enough for almost any child to own. Given the usual sources of American industrial wealth, that's not a bad legacy.

The Marx factories retooled for defense during the war; apparently, the switch from making toys to weapons is easier to accomplish than to imagine. When the plants resumed toy production, engineers were finding new applications for the vinyls and plastics that had recently been developed in response to shortages in rubber. At first, these new materials had to overcome consumer fears: when I was little, plastic toys were still being touted as not just "unbreakable" and "washable," but "non-toxic." Hard, natural rubber, which had been used in the 1930s by manufacturers like the Auburn Rubber Company to make toy cars and animals, was gradually replaced by the more flexible rubberized vinyl and, slightly later, by a variety of less expensive soft plastics. These advances made it possible to mass-produce small, virtually indestructible figurines with an impressive level of detail.

This developing technology made possible one of Marx's most distinctive and successful products, the themed playset. Although the first offering seems to have been a 1949 Outer Space set, most of the classic Marx playsets were more down-to-earth, offering miniature recreations of American life and history as filtered through the buoyant optimism of the fifties. A Marx playset typically consisted of a building or centerpiece, to be assembled from lithographed sheets of tin packed flat in the box, along with a variety of figures and accessories in vinyl or plastic—all for under $5.00. Indeed, it was the Marx playset that popularized the phrase "complete with": these flat, unassuming boxes contained everything that a child needed for recreating Fort Apache, Roy Rogers's ranch, or a WWII battlefield.

As these examples suggest, most playsets were designed for boys, for whom the term "playset figure" was immeasurably better than "doll," which these objects actually were. My friends and I would have preferred being force-fed Carter's Little Liver Pills to buying a doll. But when we saw these tiny dolls arranged in impressive dioramas in the Sears catalogue, the "wish book" of our generation, it was hard to imagine anything neater.

Francis Turner of the Moundsville museum groups Marx playsets into three broad categories: those based on historical eras and events (Prehistoric Times, Castle of the Noble Knights, the Alamo, the Blue and the Gray), on contemporary life (Airport, Service Station, Pet Shop, Cape Canaveral), and on American popular culture, especially movies and TV shows (Ben Hur, the Roy Rogers Ranch, Gunsmoke, the Untouchables). Whatever its focus, a Marx playset reflected a deft fusion of art and commerce: a well-designed toy with excellent play appeal, it was also cheap to manufacture and ship. In the factory these playsets were called "KD" or "knockdown" items: components made throughout the plant were brought together for final assembly, where they were inserted into flat boxes in a precise sequence and position to ensure a snug fit. Economic efficiencies were further enhanced by the fact that non-signature pieces could be used in a variety of playsets. Identical horses might appear in the Fort Apache and Wells Fargo sets; palm trees from the Prehistoric Times set could be reused in the Daktari Jungle.

Marx's complete-in-the-box marketing claim was not gratuitous. If you bought the Roy Rogers Rodeo Ranch for $3.79, you got the complete Roy Rogers Rodeo Ranch, right down to a cactus or two. Such a toy did not position itself as a foot in the door for future purchases in the manner of Mattel's notorious Barbie, introduced in 1959. Getting Barbie was the start of an ongoing consumer relationship. Once a little girl tired of the doll's out-of-the-box dress, the race was on: more clothes, then Ken, then Ken's clothes, then Midge, then Midge's clothes, ad infinitum. The fact that Marx playsets were mostly boys' toys makes me suspect that they contributed to the impatience with shopping that characterizes American males of my generation. I buy clothes maybe once a year, and when I do, my mission is to get in and out of the store—and preferably it *is* one store—with everything I need, complete in the box.

These playsets had iconic power. If you doubt this, consider the work of David Levinthal, a contemporary artist who has photographed Marx playset figures in striking, up-close vignettes that comment ironically on American popular culture and identity. The subtitle of his *Small Wonder: Worlds in a Box*, published in the centenary of Marx's birth, gets it exactly right. The genius of the playset lay in its capacity to stimulate the make-believe necessary to animate what David Corey calls, in an insightful introduction to Levinthal's pictures, a "hermetically complete world." As Corey observes, playsets conferred "a sense of possession" by feeding the quintessential fifties desire to "to view the world, or at least some part of it, as tidy and complete." With each playset, Marx sold a dynamic idea—a manipulable concept—rather than a static object. This was not a toy that was meant to be merely looked at, or wound up so you could watch it perform. It was you who animated the playset by arranging its various figures and accessories within and around the tin-litho building. Each playset provided the stage and characters for acting out an infinite number of stories of your devising. Naturally, this was enormously empowering: I vividly recall the feeling of control that the WWII Battleground gave me as I arranged and surveyed its little soldiers and tanks from a God's-eye view.

The worlds that Marx chose for playtime re-creation offer a telling commentary on postwar America and its obsessions. Playsets joined the movies and television in contributing to what Corey calls "the theming of America": bringing to legible clarity the image of who we were and what we wanted to be. The American Dream is often clearest—and clearest *as* a dream—to those who approach it from the outside. As the son of immigrants, Marx seems to have had an outsider's insight into these national narratives, an insight that also accounted for the commercial success of immigrants from the same culture who took up moviemaking. Marx perceived, without judgment, the underlying stories and impulses that fired the popular imagination of fifties America. In this sense, his toys were icons of icons: material embodiments of national self-images. Westward expansion, scientific exploration, America's moral example to the world, the hum of commerce, industry, and agriculture—all were celebrated in playsets that taught children the same message that Marx gave his daughter: "You are an American."

When Louis Marx retired at seventy-six, he sold the company for over fifty million dollars to Quaker Oats, which owned Fisher-Price toys. He died ten years later, on February 5, 1982, in White Plains Hospital in Westchester County. I've seen pictures of his grave, an impressive neo-Egyptian mausoleum in Woodlawn Cemetery in the Bronx. It is the tomb of a man confident of being remembered, as indeed he was. In addition to the Moundsville museum, a second Marx museum was founded in Erie in 2000 by three former employees of the Pennsylvania plants. The Toy King's name also lives on in an unrelated company called the "Marx Toy Corporation," whose copies of Marx's post-1960 action figures, introduced to compete with Hasbro's G.I. Joe, are designed primarily for the collectors' market.

Marx toys, originally so inexpensive as to be virtually disposable, are now genuine collectibles, with eBay sellers routinely including the words "Marx" and "Marx-like" in their listings even when an item has nothing to do with the company. An early-issue Prehistoric Times playset with box intact usually sells for between $150 and $250; even the later, inferior versions go for around $100. A Turnpike Service Center, originally sold by Sears in 1961, was recently snapped up with a Buy It Now for $798. Single playset figures can fetch outrageous prices too. Doc from the Gunsmoke set recently went for $223, a 54-millimeter sailor for $294, and a 45-millimeter lariat-wielding cowboy for $324. That Mao figure with Louis Marx's face recently sold for $510, and an original Marx Marx brought $250 — though mine, I'm proud to say, cost only $43 because of a stunted cigar. Even 1990s recasts of the Marx Marx are not cheap: I recently paid $25 for three of them. Low-end, widely distributed items, like most of the figures that I've been collecting, can also be pricey. A mint Ravishing Dale will usually set you back $15 to $25 — cheap at twice the price, in my view, though not everyone would agree.

In part, such prices simply reflect the scarcity of old things. But they also suggest the cultural charge that Marx playsets still carry, especially for middle-aged men. The aura surrounding vintage Marx figures might be lost on later generations, but for us, these objects are the American equivalents of Hellenistic coins and oil lamps. You can fly to Alexandria or Ephesus to see where these latter items come from, but to reach the ur-site of playset archaeology, you follow West Virginia State Route 2, which runs alongside the Ohio River, about ten miles south of Wheeling. There, just north of Moundsville, you will find the old Glen Dale factory. I made my pilgrimage three years ago, after an eBay seller from Wheeling, who knew an elderly man who had supplied the plant with Prehistoric Times boxes, confirmed that nearly all of Marx's playsets were manufactured there.

After making a right turn and heading toward the river, I found the old plant hiding in plain sight. In its heyday the Glen Dale factory employed some 2,000 people; when I saw it, it was a hulking mass of faded red brick and corrugated steel which occupied four small-town blocks along Baltimore Street. I spotted only a single hint of its former glory: an old water tower with "Marx" outlined in rust stood at the building's south end, which had housed the plastics division. As I parked, I noticed a sign above the south door proclaiming a weekend flea market; at the north end, space had been rented out to "Lesco & Co. Shipping and Receiving."

Isn't it the historian's job to get back to origins—to turn restlessness, midlife or otherwise, into knowledge that might complicate time's linear tyranny? Ignoring the "Posted: No Trespassing" signs, I walked reverently around the entire structure, testing doors and instinctively keeping an eye on the ground in a kind of surface archaeology. I half expected to spot a factory reject—perhaps a three-legged brontosaurus, or a tyrannosaurus with a grotesquely distorted face—lying hidden in the weeds and gravel. How could I not have Marx dinosaurs on my mind? After all, it was a casual eBay bid for several dinosaurs that had started me down the path that led to this lonely place. When I made my way around to the back of the factory and saw the immense loading dock that faced the river, it struck me that my old dinosaurs were once *here* before heading to my hometown Woolworth's in time for Christmas of 1955. Now everything was absolutely still: all the bustle that once filled this site had gone the way of—well, the dinosaurs.

Although an abandoned factory is not a cheerful place, the languid current of the Ohio reminded me that change is nobody's enemy, not really. I stood on the weedy riverbank and imagined thousands of Marx dinosaurs, outgrown and forgotten, drifting downstream past Cincinnati and Memphis and New Orleans until they reached the undifferentiated sea, where they would settle to the bottom and mingle with the compressed remains of their ancient, flesh-and-blood counterparts. There, of course, they would eventually become petroleum again, the source of plastic and thus, perhaps, of new toy dinosaurs yet to be conceived. Though trite, perhaps, the idea of Marx dinosaurs recycling themselves to reassert their tiny, bold presences to children yet unborn was not without its comforts.

Since making that trip, I've learned that the old plant has also been recycled—and not just in my imagination. Recently renovated into a distribution center for petroleum products, the Marx factory is humming again: ashes to ashes and oil to oil. It pleases me immensely that the old site has been turned into something new. Once the past gets unstuck, all sorts of things can start moving forward again.

Wallace Stevens once wrote that "Beauty is momentary in the mind— / The fitful tracing of a portal; / But in the flesh it is immortal." Beauty might be immortal in plastic, too. Marx figures gave me my first childhood glimpse of that species of immortality which inheres in material things whenever they are regarded with sufficient intensity and love. And don't these tough little figures persist indefinitely, as we all wish we could? Not only do these bold presences on my desktop serve as incarnations of what Americans once hoped to be, but they can also, with a slight twist of playset logic, embody what we currently *are*.

It is amusing, for instance, to imagine my English department colleagues as Marx dinosaurs. Who among us is the megatherium, powerful but clueless and thus to be avoided at all cost? Who is the pteranodon with its sidelong gaze, momentarily at rest but ready to fly off if the politics change? Or the amiable hadrosaurus, well-meaning but hopelessly out of the departmental loop? Or the grinning, toothy sphenacodon, so obviously devious as to be ineffectual? Who is the allosaurus, arms raised to request yet another research leave, and who is the startled-looking struthiomimus, too scared to request a new printer cartridge? I wisely leave unassigned the potbellied Tyrannosaurus rex, all roar and little bite—a concession, perhaps, to a measure of self-awareness.

The fantasy is ironic, as an English professor's fantasies often are, but it is also strangely reassuring. Maybe there's a Big Boy—and even a playset figure collector will concede that it might be a Big

Girl—who is studying our faces and moving us from here to there to see how we look and what we'll do. If so, let's hope that the cosmic playset owner takes better care of us than we did with our toys.

Granted, it might seem frivolous to imagine my inclusion in a Marx Liberal Arts College playset that contains a tin-litho Old Main, variously posed faculty and students, and accessories recycled from the Marx Little Red Schoolhouse. Still, it might be useful to imagine ourselves as Marx figures at 60-millimeter scale, large enough for the minute detailing of which we're usually so proud. Wasn't Louis Marx just such a "figure," someone who shaped himself in the mold of American success? And aren't we all playset figures in just this sense: plastic entities molding ourselves to whatever narratives move us? Although most of us manage to display well, we're all showing play-wear. Nearly everyone is damaged or soiled, and some of us need our "flash" trimmed. Some of us older types, cast in thick, earth-toned vinyl, resent these newer, slimmer figures in soft plastic with their gaudy primary colors. Although some people are genuine originals, most of us realize, deep down, that we are merely "re-pops" from old molds. Some of us have bases and some don't, and some of us baseless types stand upright only with difficulty.

Every story is an embodied wish. When playset stories get revised, the resulting narratives are no longer "complete in the box," but create new desires. Seekers like the Marx daughters and me would probably agree that we all want to come to life, to get picked up and moved around a little. Louis Marx may have sought this kind of liberation when he cast himself in white plastic and entered the community of small things looking for something bigger to animate them. When the magical molder of all things reduces himself to sixty millimeters, he's no longer Prospero. On the contrary, he has humbled himself to become one toy among many, a portly man with a cigar who could be chatting with cowboy drifters and dull-witted dinosaurs—not just presidents and generals—if things were so arranged. Haven't I taken the Marx Marx from his usual place in the second row of this crowd, and isn't he conversing, at this very moment, with a fierce-looking frontiersman and an indifferent woolly mammoth?

The flesh-and-blood Louis Marx would have had little patience with such strained profundities. Still, he might have understood the visceral charge that comes from holding a mint brontosaurus in flat gray, weary-faced but ready for anything, just like Standing Roy and Ravishing Dale. Marx might even share my excitement at spotting a megatherium and iguanodon in flat tan with only twenty-three minutes left in the auction. Having become the proud owner of all the toy dinosaurs I need, assuming I really needed any of them, still I tell myself that bidding on these figures would be a perfectly rational act. It might bring me two steps closer to having the complete second series of dinosaurs in tan, which might in turn bring contentment—and what self-respecting seeker could shun the possibility of that?

Animal Husbandry . . . .

O f the playset animals scattered throughout the desktop crowd, three—a horse, a dog, and a dinosaur—are standing in the second row, just behind the multiple Roys and Dales and only a trot away from Louis Marx himself. The horse and the dog are inevitable: how could Roy's faithful companions not be close at hand? Bullet, ears erect and tongue lolling in a canine smile, sits bolt upright and awaits a new command, while a white vinyl Trigger stands nearby, proudly unencumbered by saddle or reins. It is the dinosaur positioned between them, however, that holds pride of place. Cast in soft gray plastic, this Marx allosaurus—"Al" for short—is the designated Chief Animal of my figure collection. Al is a revered reminder of playset origins, a patriarch of First Things.

In the beginning was the dinosaur—a statement that holds true not just for my collecting life, which progressed from dinosaurs to other animals to people, but for my real life. Fourteen Marx dinosaurs were the first playset figures that I owned as a child. These variously shaped grotesques had a two-year jump on my original Roy and Dale, both of whom, once they arrived, wound up cavorting as often in the Jurassic as in the American West. Standing Roy routinely rescued Ravishing Dale from the tyrannosaurus's extended claws with little more than a cool gaze; Sitting Roy rode the Marx brontosaurus more often than he rode Trigger. Although I eventually owned other toy animals, mostly farm and jungle sets made by the Auburn Rubber company, they never saw much play. Marx dinosaurs remained my favorites until I outgrew such toys altogether.

It's no accident that I found dinosaurs—both the toys and the real things—more interesting than living animals. My father grew up on a farm, and had the country boy's classic distaste for animals in the house. When I was around age four, my older sister prevailed against Dad's objections and got two cats, which I barely remember except for their grisly end. After Snowball and Snooks got flattened on Ohio Route 15, Sue vowed never to get hurt like that again and joined Dad in maintaining a pet-free house. Absences beg to be filled, and I filled this one with fear. There were no leash laws in our town, and a pet-less boy unable to read animal faces couldn't know whether a strange dog heading his way was friendly or fierce. Though never bitten, I was often chased—probably needlessly, because I knew nothing of animal play; had I simply stood still, I might have made a shaggy friend or two. I paid a steep price for my timidity. Not only did I grow up without knowing the joys of animal companionship, but I missed out on the two great insights that animals can provide: empathy with creatures different from us, and an awareness of another, more visceral way of experiencing the world.

My fear of animals did not stop me from being curious about them. This curiosity prompted my first remembered act of compensation: a boy who wants to learn about animals but is afraid to get near them might well seek a substitute in toy animals—and if he wants to play it double-safe, they will be toy animals whose real-world counterparts cannot possibly harm him. Thus began a longstanding devotion to plastic dinosaurs. The knowledge that I would never see a flesh-and-blood dinosaur allowed me to play with Al and his companions with a light heart, cheerfully filling their real-world absence with play-world stories that didn't involve getting chased, bitten, or eaten. By masking my fear of real animals, Marx dinosaurs made me feel braver and more adventurous than I actually was. After my sister pronounced them creepy, they possessed bad-boy appeal even within our house, where no dog could get at me.

I regret this deeply; nowadays I find it inconceivable to live without a pet. Bullet's prominence on this desktop is less a concession to Roy than an apology to all the animal friends that I never made as a child. My shift from animal fear to animal love didn't start until graduate school, when my girlfriend and I found a litter of black and white kittens that had been abandoned in a nearby junkyard. After placing all but one with a local farmer, we named the remaining kitten Left-Mark after a black mark on the left side of her otherwise white snout. The human relationship lasted four years; the one with the cat, sixteen—from my late twenties to my early forties. A Marx Pet Shop cat poised on my desk, its tail raised and its head pointing warily to the side, is aping a remembered Left-Mark gait.

While the Pet Shop cat evokes an animal bond from the past, Bullet celebrates a bond that resides squarely in the present. His alert bearing reminds me of our dog Henry, a Hungarian puli bred to herd sheep and, apparently, to be incapable of remaining still for more than five minutes at a time. While Bullet's pose never changes, Henry's is never the same. Even his sleep is fitful, punctuated by theatrical sighs and frequent repositionings, always with a scuttle of claws on the hardwood floor followed by a decisive flop. Though Henry is getting old, he still quivers with excitement at the slightest smell, sound, or movement, jerking his head and darting his eyes to gauge where to direct his bark. I can watch this dog for a long time without getting bored, although I do so furtively because being watched makes him even jumpier than usual. There's often a measure of envy in my gaze: Henry seems to know things that I don't.

Having overcome my boyhood terror, I've probably gone too far in the other direction: now I can't help romanticizing animals as shaggy sages, philosophers of nonhuman experience. Animals dwell in a sensory world of which we have only the dullest acquaintance, trapped as we are within a web of words and ideas and thus living at several removes from physical reality. It's difficult to look at the toy animals that I've collected without imagining that they, too, possess this inaccessible wisdom. Bullet, an inch and a half from his rump to the tip of his peaked ears, seems attuned to even tinier stimuli than Henry is: if Henry does physics at an observable level, Bullet deals in quantum mechanics.

However strange it might be to envy one's dog, I envy Henry for the same reason that I envy the 60-millimeter people standing on my desk. Although their faces and forms resemble mine, their stubborn materiality—I read it as defiance—makes them seem to inhabit the world more aggressively than I do. They assert themselves with bracing clarity: a soldier is unmistakably a soldier, a cowboy a cowboy, a knight a knight. It's easy to fantasize scenarios in which these figures stage covert rodeos, disco contests, and footraces around the laptop. Their ceaseless activity must make me look hopelessly inert. I imagine them wondering what's up with the sluggish giant who keeps staring

at them: that big sleepwalker who looks so indistinct and tentative—
what's *he* supposed to be? Protective of their animal-like connection
with a reality more concrete than mine, they have conspired to shut
me out. My sudden glances never catch anyone off guard: every time
I look, they stop moving.

This illusion of suspended animation is especially powerful in the
toy animals. A playset animal is a plastic object that replicates a fleshly
object with hyper-connections to the physical world. How could a
middle-aged academic, especially a latecomer to animal appreciation, not hope to make up for lost time by experiencing some of that
hyper-connecting for himself? I cannot help harboring an absurd,
Dr. Dolittle daydream of talking to animals about animal otherness,
about how they see the world. If language and culture haven't permanently shut me out, maybe I can see it that way, too—provided
that I can atone for some childhood cowardice. Such atonement will
not come easily: even the Marx allosaurus, one of my earliest playset
companions, issues a soft-plastic reproach by standing perfectly still
and keeping his nonhuman secrets to himself. In his stern silence, Al
almost makes me forget that I'm the one who's supposed to be in
charge here, that this is *my* desktop world.

The Marx company introduced its Prehistoric Times playset in 1955.
Complete with a vacuum-formed landscape, palm trees, cavemen, and
fourteen dinosaurs in flat gray or green, the set cost $4.89. Historical
hindsight makes it easy to see why this item was so popular. Meshing
nicely with the postwar infatuation with science, dinosaurs offered a
backward-gazing flipside to the era's preoccupation with outer space:
just as astronomy was revealing the future, paleontology was revealing
the past. The impact of Marx dinosaurs on the popular imagination
was lasting. Since their appearance, along with the 1953 *Life* magazine
series on prehistoric animals that inspired them, every generation has
had its childhood love affair with dinosaurs, both the toys and the
real things. Walk into any Wal-Mart and you can still find plastic dinosaurs, now made mostly in China and packaged in clear tubes.

Although I never owned the Prehistoric Times playset, Marx also
sold their dinosaurs in small packs and loose in dime-store bins. Al
and his scaly companions came into my life, without landscape, trees,
or cavemen, on Christmas of 1955, when I was two weeks shy of turn-

ing six. The company brought out a second series of eight new figures in 1961, including three extinct mammals, but I never saw them. If I had, they would have been impossible to resist.

The fact that dinosaurs lived solely in my imagination made it easy to embrace their toy counterparts not only as danger-free animals, but as affable playmates. It is impossible, even today, to look at the fourteen figures that I owned without conjuring up the personalities that I once imposed on them. The Tyrannosaurus rex, with its sheer bulk and menacing fangs, was clearly the boss of the group even though its grimace could be read as a smile; its ferocity was further softened by a protruding belly and an oddly static pose, with one arm raised in a tentative wave. The brontosaurus, with its unruffled expression and long, graceful neck, was a gentle giant—a born pacifist. The kronosaurus, the only aquatic animal in the set, looked sneaky; its smooth skin contrasted with the pebbled or cross-hatched texture of the other figures, and its open mouth could be squeezed to make it "talk." Every Marx dinosaur possessed just this sort of character, an effect enhanced by the presence of the animal's name and length on its belly or tail. The low-headed stegosaurus was a stubborn dullard; the pointy-beaked pteranodon, a nervous Nellie. The plateosaurus, small and sad-faced, looked lonely, so he often shared a pocket—the lucky lizard—with Ravishing Dale. My favorite, of course, was the deeply-pebbled allosaurus, whose quizzical expression and raised forearms made him look as if he were about to ask a favor.

The pudgy, tentative Al offered a perfect blend of human personality and animal mystery. This duality characterized all the Marx dinosaurs: although they evoked sufficient personalities to imagine them as odd-looking people, they were too "realistic" to be humanized completely. Their exotic appeal was inseparable from the fact that they were not cute—a fact that my sister was quick to point out. With their reptilian bodies and poses, they were unmistakably lizards, which made them harder to read than the cowboys, presidents, and army men that came later. Their faces kept oscillating between the human traits that I projected onto them and a relentless animality that kept them mysterious.

Their position in time was equally paradoxical. I loved my toy dinosaurs despite my awareness that their real-life counterparts were "extinct," a fancy word for "all dead." This stark fact sometimes bothered me, not least because it forced me out of make-believe into the realization that my plastic pets weren't real—that the actual dinosaurs had all died just as surely as Curly the stooge and James Dean had died. But children at play will often find a bright edge even to sad things. In my case, the cheering antidote came from a half-formed notion that by playing with these toys, I was somehow keeping the actual dinosaurs alive. I was too invested in the reality of dinosaurs to imagine them utterly gone: maybe they weren't really and truly dead so long as I had my toy dinosaurs and took good care of them.

If I were to translate this childhood superstition into adult terms, I'd say that Marx dinosaurs taught me that memory is as tangible as anything else in the world—that absences can be embodied in presences, even if those presences are molded in soft plastic. It's even possible that I loved my dinosaurs *because* they were dead. Remembering the sad fate of Snowball and Snooks, I was terrified at the thought that my parents might follow my sister's cats out of the world. But just as I was beginning to absorb this dark possibility, Marx dinosaurs stepped in with their weird, living-and-dead doubleness to confirm that the past stayed alive for whoever bothered to remember it.

Other playset figures that I owned as a child reinforced this notion, especially the Marx presidents. I knew that only six of these thirty-six figures (Hoover, Truman, two Ikes, and two Mamies) represented living people—yet here they all were, the dead and the living standing together in gleaming white plastic, aggressively present and ready for play. The real Roy Rogers and Dale Evans were alive, too, and so were my cowboys and soldiers. As my extinct dinosaurs and dead presidents mingled with these "living" figures, they seemed supremely unruffled by their own deaths. When your play involves Honest Abe and Quizzical Al vying for the hand of Ravishing Dale, who is secretly in love not with Standing Roy but with the dapper William McKinley, the scary divide between the living and the dead will get blurred a little. I did not consciously grasp this, of course, but its comfort was as tangible as a Marx brontosaurus, wonderfully grippable in textured plastic.

Thus began a lifelong attraction to the past. A literary historian studies old texts and tries to reanimate the people who wrote them—

not so different, really, from a six-year-old peering into the inscrutable face of an extinct allosaurus and seeking a story there. Although my adult profession did not stem exclusively from Louis Marx, I should acknowledge the initial push: his dinosaurs helped turn me into the sort of child who might grow up to teach old literature in an English department. Indeed, the first written text that I can remember deciphering was molded into a dinosaur's tail: "TYRANNOSAURUS." Thanks to eBay, I can now flip the T. rex over and reread my second text: "50' LONG." Reading came early to me because I wanted to learn as much about these ancient creatures as I could. In second grade I was paraded through our school and made to read aloud from what had become my favorite book, *All About Dinosaurs* by Roy Chapman Andrews. My sister, who cringed with embarrassment when this freak show came to her sixth-grade class, owes Louis Marx a different sort of thanks.

As Sue could tell you, beloved animals die. By playing with Marx dinosaurs, a child could grasp this disturbing truth from a comfortable distance because these animals were already dead. They brought none of that horrible suspense—when and how will Spot die?—that comes with owning a pet. I've since discovered that other playset animals can also ease the twin terrors of time and mortality. In its rubbery permanence, the Pet Shop cat could be the Archetypal Cat that exists in Plato's realm of pure forms, of which Left-Mark was a time-bound and thus fallen copy. This playset cat reminds me of the soothing effect that watching Left-Mark always had on me. Today I get this same tranquility from observing Henry's commitment to his routines and his earnest readiness for Anything To Happen. To gaze at this dog feels like I imagine prayer feels to a religious person. And why not? Animals *know* things.

Toy animals seem to know things, too—and for me, Marx dinosaurs remain the sagest of the sage, the Bertrand Russells and Albert Einsteins of the playset animals that I've collected. These plastic reptiles, all going about their business, provoke something of the meditative calm that comes from observing real animals and noting their lofty indifference to us. To paraphrase Whitman, "I think I could turn and live awhile with Marx dinosaurs, they are so placid and self-contained, I stand and look at them sometimes half the day long." The payoff of so prolonged a gaze is obvious: you'll never catch a dinosaur—or any other animal, for that matter—sleepwalking or looking indistinct. Their connection with the world is far too direct for that.

Although the flesh-and-blood dinosaurs died off too early to teach us this lesson, their mammalian successors must have provoked a similar sense of otherness among our distant ancestors, who could not become self-aware as humans unless there were sentient beings around that were *not* human. The concept of divinity may also have stemmed from a recognition of the nonhuman power and beauty of animals. The unstated truce between pets and their owners—a pledge, basically, not to eat one another—is an ancient covenant. Its Stone Age version, sealed with bits of meat tossed into the darkness beyond the campfire, must have offered precedent for those other covenants in which we promised to worship the gods and they promised not to destroy us. The human/animal bond dates from a time when we loved our prey as much as Left-Mark loved hers. Why else would our Paleolithic forebears paint their victims so lovingly on cave walls that could be seen only after claustrophobic crawls through dank tunnels? Bringing the brilliance of fire into these dark, airless places, we applied ochre and charcoal to the sacred task of rendering the contours of that which gave us life. The animal-headed deities of ancient Egypt reflected a desire for even greater intimacy with this otherness. To place a hawk's head on a man's body was to imagine the divine as a blend of human and animal essences: the gods, we figured, must be a little like us and a little like them.

As windows to such mysteries, the playset animals positioned on this desktop might not be all that different from the painted animals that adorn Paleolithic caves and Egyptian tombs. The Marx Pet Shop cat freezes the stealthy tread of the eternal predator, whose engagement with the physical world defines the difference between starving and not starving. I used to observe that tread in Left-Mark as she enacted predatory instincts that remained untamed even in a so-called "domestic" shorthair. Nowadays I see it in Henry: even his play is a pastiche of the primordial impulses that kept his ancestors alive. This dog embodies the antithesis of the human habit of living almost entirely within our heads. And although Quizzical Al has no living counterpart to show me this realm, his bulging eyes convince me that if it weren't for the pesky fact of extinction, his prototype would also have made an excellent guide. It is difficult to imagine the mysterious imperatives of Al's instinct-driven world without wanting to go there, if only for a while.

The second series of Marx prehistoric animals contained five dino-saurs—styracosaurus, struthiomimus, iguanodon, parasaurolophus, and moschops—and three mammals: the megatherium, the woolly mammoth, and the proto-Left-Mark smilodon with its outlandish fangs. I never saw these figures as a child, and they evoke no memo-ries. Still, they are impressive by any standard. The mammoth in par-ticular, especially in the early-issue flat plastic, is almost heartbreak-ing in its purity of execution. The initial designs for both series were in fact so good that only minimal changes were made during their twenty-odd years of production: a revised allosaurus does not lean so far to one side; a revised triceratops has daintier horns; a revised trachodon stands straighter and has new arm positions. The one ma-jor change was the demise of the bearer of my first reading matter. The ferocious yet harmless potbellied T. rex was replaced in 1961 by a more anatomically probable tyrannosaurus that strides purposefully with its tail whipping around. The reptilian body and scaly texture of the revised T. rex are so convincing that they hardly seem possible in plastic; it and the mammoth are among the best animal figures that Marx ever made.

As I study the Marx dinosaurs now, I am struck by the beauty that inheres in any well-made thing. Clearly, the people who produced these figures put a great deal of time and care into their design. An especially renowned figure designer during the fifties was Floyd "Joe" Chamberlain, a Glen Dale boy who went to work at the plant soon after high school. Walter Nisperly, another local boy with no college experience but a lot of talent, joined the model room in 1939 and eventually became head of the Design and Development department, which at its peak employed some thirty-five artists and model-makers. Although the commercial nature of the enterprise might prompt some to see these men as mere technicians, I have no hesitation in calling them artists. What is art, after all, but an impulse to go beyond mere function and need, to make a thing better than it has to be? If the close-grained pebbling on the skin of the Marx iguanodon doesn't embody the artistic compulsion to transcend sheer necessity, I don't know what does.

Sometimes "art" is most discernable in contrast to that which is clearly *not* art. When the Multiple Products Corporation issued a series of toy dinosaurs in the mid-1960s, just as Marx was suspending production of their own line, most of the MPC figures copied the Marx versions right down to the poses. In contrast to the meticulous detailing and generous heft of Marx's figures, however, the MPC dinosaurs were vague and thin, requiring fewer molds, less plastic, and infinitely less imagination. What these copies chiefly missed was a subtle dualism: while the Marx dinosaurs artfully positioned themselves somewhere between toys and replicas, the MPC dinosaurs were just toys, and cheap ones at that. The Marx versions were reasonably faithful representations that could nonetheless be played with like toys. Although they were sufficiently realistic to let you know that they were animals, and therefore not you, their quasi-expressive faces and poses made it clear that they were playthings waiting to be animated by stories that *were* you. A cultural theorist would say that every Marx dinosaur walked a line between representation and performance, between an object transparent to something behind it—that is, a real dinosaur—and an object that is readable only on its own terms, as itself. Today's toy dinosaurs lack this wonderful ambiguity. Some of the recent figures are like museum replicas: skillfully designed and paleontologically accurate, but no longer toys. Others have gone the route of Barney: plush, large-headed, and cuddly. Although these are clearly toys, they are no longer dinosaurs.

If the realism of Marx dinosaurs got me hooked on the past, their toyness made bearable my recognition that the past was gone and the real dinosaurs were dead. Theater people know that artifice, when frankly acknowledged, can conjure a reality deeper than can be evoked by more naturalistic modes of performance. If as a child you anthropomorphized your Marx dinosaurs, as their varied characters demanded, they also made it clear that you—and you alone—were the source of their personalities and adventures. That's a substantial imaginative burden, but once accepted, it empowered you to make up your own stories. What more can be asked of a toy than that?

As a child I tried, with mixed success, to overcome my fear of animals by confronting the specimens on annual display at the Hancock County Fair. The cattle were impossibly huge, like those bulls from

Crete in my mother's art book, and their languid movements seemed to imitate the slow-motion gait of the unclassifiable beasts that chased me in nightmares. The steers provoked special awe. After my father told me how they became steers, I kept sneaking glances between their hind legs, looking for some horrible wound. The pigs, large and bristly and nothing like cartoon pigs, were even scarier than the cows. The playset pigs that I have acquired capture something of the sullen intelligence that I remember seeing on the faces in those pens: while the Auburn Rubber pig looks disgruntled, the Poland China sow from the Marx Prize Livestock set looks bemused. By contrast, the vinyl pig included in Marx's earliest farm sets seems to be smiling. This must be what William Cullen Bryant meant by nature's "various language." The affability of the early Marx pig convinces me that if I had owned the Happi-Time Farm as a child, I would have had one less species to be afraid of.

The Marx dinosaurs need no such rehabilitation; after all, their flesh-and-blood prototypes were already long gone. And isn't it always the absent thing that makes the heart grow fonder? As a child I could ride my bike out of town and, within fifteen minutes, see real cows and pigs. But precisely because real dinosaurs lay beyond the realm of seeing, I could fill their absence with whatever stories I wanted. I'm not alone in this impulse. As the persistence of Sasquatch, the yeti, and the Loch Ness monster suggests, our deepest and most satisfying imaginings are sparked by fantasy animals, the animals of pure desire. Because something in us *wants* the unicorn, the Minotaur, and the dragon to exist, they, like the dinosaurs, will never die off. To put this in toy terms, the unseen animal has exceptional play value because it poses a real-world void that begs to be filled with the imagination. It requires an unusual blend of discipline and vision to invest everyday animals with this kind of imaginative power. Zoologists can do this, and maybe a few poets. Most children can do it, too, but I was not among them because I was too scared to try.

Like everything else under the playset sun, the Marx dinosaurs suffered a fall. Both series were sold loose and in playsets through 1964, and when their production resumed in the early seventies, they were cast in cheap, waxy plastic. But weren't the seeds of this final indignity sown at the very beginning? The quasi-educational figures that I loved were already sullied, not only by the inclusion of those anachronistic cavemen in Prehistoric Times playsets, but also by the sensationalistic label that sometimes appeared on their header cards: "Prehistoric Monsters." The slide continued into the sixties, when the company included dinosaurs in the Flintstones and One Million Years B.C. playsets, both of which reflected the increasing tie-in of Marx toys with TV shows and movies. The bright, garish colors of the later figures also reflected an industry-wide trend mandated by color television. When Robert Frost asked us "what to make of a diminished thing," he could have been holding a post-1971 brontosaurus in waxy yellow.

Science itself would eventually antiquate my old toys, as is clear from an informative and amusing Web site called Realm of Rubber Dinosaurs. The anonymous webmaster points out that most of the Marx figures did not represent specific dinosaurs but broad types, zoological genera at best. The trachodon, for instance, was a generalized duckbill rather than a particular species: its closest equivalent is now called edmontosaurus. The peace-loving brontosaurus—a similar dinosaur is now called apatosaurus—never existed: like the *Life* illustration on which it was based, the Marx brontosaurus followed a faulty skeletal reconstruction that placed the wrong head on the body. Other Marx figures are no longer classified as dinosaurs at all, but as proto-mammals (dimetrodon, sphenacodon, cynognathus, moschops, and kronosaurus) and a proto-bird (pteranodon). Like the facts of history and science, my beloved toys were more provisional than I knew.

I suffered a fall, too, when I turned eleven or twelve and stopped playing with my dinosaurs altogether. Like evolution personified, I left them behind, not in a stratum of sedimentary rock but in a bedroom closet, where they stayed until they presumably lumbered off in the same yard sale that took Roy and Dale. My current regret at their disappearance is not about monetary loss, with old toys as stand-ins for baseball cards ("Imagine what they would be worth today!"), but about duty. I should have honored my dinosaurs for the hours of joy that they once gave me. I should have taken care of them.

Most toy collectors feel this guilt. Beneath our hobbyist's buoyancy, we know that old toys embody loss. As children we loved these objects unaware that we would someday leave them behind; as adults we can't look at them without mourning the children whom we left behind by growing up. For me, playset animals evoke this sense of loss with special poignancy. Genesis commanded us to "have dominion over the fish of the sea, and over the birds of the air, and over the cattle, and over all the wild animals of the earth, and over every creeping thing that creeps upon the earth." Ranchers, farmers, and furriers might cite these words as a divine endorsement of what they do, but doesn't the verse also imply that we should take care of our animals, whether flesh and blood or plastic? If so, I have much to answer for: Marx dinosaurs were once my stand-ins for pets, and to abandon a pet is as irresponsible an act as I can imagine.

For a lover and loser of toy animals, however, faith is the evidence of things not seen—that is, until those things actually *are* seen. Isn't Quizzical Al once again standing before me, along with Bullet, Trigger, and the Pet Shop cat? And aren't dozens of their fellows—the Marx and Auburn woodland creatures, the Marx and MPC jungle sets, the three Marx farm sets, and the Marx Prize Livestock—safely tethered nearby in plastic bags? Belated repentance for childhood fear and indifference can perhaps be enacted on this very desktop: a Hong Kong lion can lie down with an Auburn Rubber lamb, benignly overseen by Simon the Zealot from the Marx apostles set—the one playset figure in a thousand that faintly resembles me.

At least one thing is certain—no vintage toys are better suited for investing everyday animals with dinosaur-like beauty than the Marx Prize Livestock: the stalwart Clydesdale, too magnificent even for Sitting Roy to sully with an impertinent ride; the delicate Brown Swiss, with her textured coat and snaking udder veins; the American Shorthorn bull standing foursquare in defiant bulk and substance. The aesthetic appeal of these toys matters a great deal, because it reinforces another notion that my dinosaurs gave me as a child: the soothing possibility that animals, like art, might last forever. The fear of time's impact on our pets—always an inflected fear of its impact on *us*—might be eased by reaffirming our forebears' belief in animal immortality. Didn't those Paleolithic hunters keep taking deer that looked identical to ones that they had already killed and eaten? We now know, of course, that animals are just as vulnerable to time and change as we are. This is why I routinely liberate their playset counterparts from the temporal strictures of biological history. When a Marx woolly mammoth and an Auburn Rubber elephant regard each other warily, evolutionary time has been transcended, at least for the moment.

The comforts of this vignette are obvious: aren't we all—man and beast alike—caught up in the same rush toward oblivion? The Marx company conceded as much in 1971, when it issued an Animal Kingdom series under the aegis of the World Wildlife Fund. A cynic might lament the petroleum that went into the set's production and the pollution that its manufacture released into the Ohio River as it flowed past the Glen Dale plant. What's more, each animal came in its own cardboard box: that's a lot of trees felled in the interest of environmental awareness. And how much money spent on Animal Kingdom sets might have gone directly to environmental research? Still, Rachel Carson's *Silent Spring* had been out for less than a decade, and it took years for her message to gain its still-growing hold on the national consciousness. I have no doubt that Marx's intentions in producing the Animal Kingdom were honorable. I even suspect that the set created its share of future zoologists, biologists, and ecologists.

Had the Animal Kingdom figures been around when I was little, I might have gotten a jump on learning a lesson that had to wait until my old cat taught it to me: we mammals are all first cousins—and the cliché about pets being "part of the family" is more accurate than I ever knew. At least I know it now. Whenever I scratched Left-Mark's chin and she extended her head in full stretch, didn't she reveal the rat-like face of the generic ur-mammal whose features we can still trace in the mirror?

Although Left-Mark died seventeen years ago, I still have an occasional dream in which I see her floating through interstellar space, fortified only by her instincts and that last meal of Purina. As I watch her follow some unknown directive, I'm grateful that she shared some of her nonhuman magic with a fellow mammal who is far more domesticated than she could ever be. Henry's vestigial wildness now provides the same bracing counter to those mental structures which dull our capacity to experience life through the body: the warmth of sunbeams, the ecstasy of food, the spiraling dance of dust-motes. A realm so described might sound like an unattainable fantasy; doesn't being human mean that we no longer live chiefly by our senses? But while we can't go home again, a dog and a cat can take us a little closer, provided that we come when they call and are sufficiently wise to follow their lead.

This, too, is a desktop lesson. Although the flesh-and-blood allosaurus is long gone, Quizzical Al remains to bear witness to a wide-eyed, saurian experience of the world. The flesh-and-blood Henry, currently napping downstairs, is imperfectly embodied in soft-plastic Bullet—imperfectly because if Bullet had been a puli, half of every Roy Rogers episode would have consisted of Roy yelling "No bark! No bark!" Left-Mark is here, too, along with my sister's feline sacrifices to Route 15, in their Pet Shop avatar. A playset cat, if it isn't discarded or destroyed, will outlast a real cat every time. The recognition that this also goes for people might make a middle-aged man gazing at fifty-year-old toys feel that his own slide toward extinction is moving a little too quickly. While such a man could waste his remaining days flinching at the darkness beyond the campfire, he might instead resolve to live more fully in what's left of his animal senses—to engage more directly with what's right in front of him.

Right in front of me, at this moment, is a complete set of Marx Pet Shop dogs that I've retrieved from their bag. These figures are excellent contemplative objects for any would-be animal who longs to tap into nonhuman experience. A real animal, however, will need no such crutches. This was recently confirmed when Henry encountered these figures, which were set up on the living room floor. It didn't seem to bother him that the set does not include a puli. Given his temperament, a Marx puli would probably irritate him: he would judge its body too scrawny and its pose stiff and unconvincing. Or more likely, he would conclude that it was merely a small object that could be neither eaten nor loved. When Henry encountered his playset counterparts, he sniffed them briefly—*Nothing here!*—and trotted off, eschewing the oily smell of rubberized vinyl for a more enticing scent, wafting from somewhere else, that was lost on me.

No Time Like the Present

Roy and Dale did not enter my seven-year-old world alone, but arrived with fourteen Mineral City residents, now known to collectors as the "town" cowboys to distinguish them from the "ranch" cowboys and the "rodeo" cowboys that came with other playsets. Thanks to eBay, all of the Mineral Citizens are once again standing before me. Unlike the gleaming white Rogerses, these figures were cast in yellowish rubberized vinyl. But there is another difference: while Roy and Dale look completely at ease, the agitated poses of the townsfolk reflect another mood altogether. An angry cowboy delivers an uppercut; the recipient of this punch, his head snapped back, has fallen to the ground. One sheriff holds a bag of recovered loot as he arrests a sad-faced outlaw who does a cowboy perp-walk with raised arms. A second sheriff with a wary expression brandishes a pistol in each hand; a crouching, grim-faced cowboy cradles a removable rifle; another scofflaw turns at the hips and fans his pistol; a masked, mounted bandit fires back at his pursuers. Nor does Mineral City danger come solely from guns: a frantic, open-mouthed rider flails his arms as he falls from his horse.

The contrast between the stately Rogerses and nearly everyone else gives Mineral City a split personality; it is a place where comfort and terror coexist. The townsfolk include only five apparent pacifists: a lassoing rider; a bonneted lady carrying a basket; a loping man—her husband?—holding a harness; a man mounting a horse, no doubt to flee this chaotic place; and a seated man in chaps who waves and flashes a silly, Alfred E. Neuman grin. He looks happy—and why not? He is as oblivious to the surrounding turmoil as the town's First Couple.

The fact that Mineral City is a cauldron of fear for two-thirds of its populace raises issues of playset morality. Although the real Roy and Dale were constantly telling us kids to don the white hats of good guys, their playset avatars seem callously indifferent to the violence that surrounds them. Indeed, their placid smiles suggest that they might even be amused by it. The town's two sheriffs are doing their best to keep the peace, but how, exactly, are Roy and Dale helping out? And why are they dwelling in this lawless place to begin with? To be fair, Aggressive Roy, grim-faced and with gun drawn, looks more than ready to step up, but he didn't come with my childhood set. I had only two smiling Roys and one smiling Dale by which to gauge the town's moral compass, and they were no help at all.

Studying these figures now, I'd say that the Mineral City playset embodied an odd sort of anachronism: the untroubled conflation of an Old West, where nameless people shoot and get shot, and a New West where celebrities smile for the camera. We kids knew that Roy and Dale were modern people: weren't they on TV every week, and didn't their sidekick Pat Brady drive a Jeep? The other Mineral Citizens, by contrast, inhabited an earlier era that offered little to smile about. This temporal confusion is especially evident in the town's two women. While Dale's fancy, star-studded outfit would be a fitting choice for the Country Music Awards, the bonneted matron, with her floor-length dress and apron tied with a large bow, has a decidedly Victorian look. Why would the Marx designers, ordinarily sticklers for research and realism, so blatantly violate the "unities," that principle of classical theater which insists that the time and place of all dramatic action be consistent?

My guess is that they did so in order to render the Old West safe for play. If Roy and Dale existed in the child's here and now, then so did their unflappability. The unruffled ease of the town's First Couple brought the untamed West into the carefree present of play, where nothing bad could ever happen. We kids knew from TV and the movies that the actual Old West had been like a school playground filled with bullies—only much, much bigger. Mineral City countered the anxieties of this place by putting us in charge of it. Indeed, the playset's chief appeal lay in this control: for all the gunplay, people never got wounded unless you made them wounded by knocking them over. Such reassurance was reinforced by the fact that the antic townsfolk were resilient—and literally so: although the terrified bronco rider could never relax, he could fall all day and never get hurt. Even if you staged a Mineral City Armageddon, pelting the town with Ping-Pong balls or paper wads until no one was left standing, everybody would be ready to rumble the next time you played with them. Within Mineral City's eternal present, nothing was so bad as to be irreversible—not even time's scariest emissary, death.

Through it all, Roy and Dale kept smiling, blissfully above the fray. What's more, the child who identified with them was even higher above the fray. The logic behind the First Couple's inappropriate smiles becomes clear if you can remember—or imagine—playing with Mineral City. Secure in the knowledge that you were partnered with Roy and Dale in the playset present, you would be smiling, too. Had there been a mirror nearby, you might have noticed that your mindless grin resembled theirs as you walked them into the saloon for Cokes despite the surrounding mayhem. You might even have resembled those children playing with Marx toys in the Sears Christmas catalogue, the ones who could smile without crinkling their eyes.

Pat Brady was above the fray, too. The Old West anarchy enacted by the townsfolk did not impede his New West access to the Jeep dealership where he must have acquired Nellybelle, perhaps with a loan co-signed by Roy. The Jeep provided an additional hint of present security as an antidote to historical danger. Mineral City came with hitching posts and watering troughs for the horses, but no gas pump or lube rack for Nellybelle—a subtle but effective endorsement of the fifties present. Wouldn't a maintenance-free car create a profound faith in modern times?

Every Marx playset that depicted an historical era or event offered a similar buffer against the more disturbing aspects of history. We small fifties people learned from these even smaller plastic people that we could control the past and our contacts with it: these toys could take us there whenever we chose, but always with a promise of safe return. The advertisement in the Sears catalogue for the Prehistoric Times playset made this explicit by inviting kids to "take off in your Time Machine." The ad copy was seductive in the extreme: "There's a dizzying sensation as it hovers over your home—and suddenly the buildings are gone. Instead, you see forest landscape below. Palms and ferns are everywhere." What bored child could resist this sweeping away of mundanity—all the chalk dust, shoelaces, and meatloaf of everyday life suddenly gone? At the same time, such escapes ultimately reaffirmed the child's ordinary world as the safest of places in the best of times.

Such postwar optimism was widespread; it also accounted for the prestige of the educational toy. What were historical playsets if not vehicles for learning about the past under the painless guise of play? And didn't history prove, time and again, how lucky we kids were to be living today? Any king of the mountain, of course, must defend the summit: learning through play appealed to parents who were convinced that if American children weren't smart, the Russians would beat us. Historical playsets taught us what we would be fighting for. They extolled the American present by simultaneously confronting us with—and insulating us from—the ongoing turmoil of other times and places, including some very distant ones. The Prehistoric Times set, that self-styled "time machine" which included dinosaurs and palm trees, could not yield its lessons unless little versions of us were there to learn them. This "educational" playset included tiny cavemen in six poses, even though dinosaurs and humans missed each other by sixty million years. In playset prehistory, narrative desire trumped paleontological fact: putting dinosaurs and humans together produced a more legible and uplifting story. History, as Marx playsets portrayed it, was consistently and profoundly upbeat; how could it be otherwise, when its final product was us?

History also had a dramatic sweep to it. Close on the heels of dinosaurs and Neanderthals came the Bible, represented by playset versions of Noah's ark, the Ten Commandments, the Nativity, and Jesus and the apostles. Antiquity was also depicted in 60-millimeter figure sets of Egyptians and Romans, each in eight agitated, warlike poses. Noah's ark, with its little pairs of animals, was a playset natural—though only so peaceful if you ignored all the drowned people who did not come with the set. The Ten Commandments playset was among many which proved that good times and good business went hand in hand. Children who hadn't gotten enough of Charlton Heston's nuanced performance in the 1956 movie could prolong it on the living room floor. However crass the tie-in to Hollywood might now seem to baby boomers, who routinely idealize our childhoods as a time before "everything got commercialized," this was precisely the origin of my beloved Roy and Dale—and they were only the beginning.

When Heston starred in *Ben Hur* three years later, Marx followed suit with a set that focused not on the tensions between Romans and Jews or the rise of Christianity, like the book and movie, but on the gory chariot race. This set came complete with three character figures: in addition to a vaguely Hestonian Ben Hur, an emperor and an empress held stately poses that echoed those of Roy and Dale, elite observers who stood above the fray, at modern ease despite their toga and gown. Playset history jumped from ancient Rome to a cheerful mingling of the Dark and Middle Ages, in playsets of knights, Vikings, and two Robin Hood sets at 60-millimeter and 54-millimeter scales. Here, the elite role was played most openly by Friar Tuck, whose 60-millimeter version observes the surrounding mayhem with frank glee.

Given the Vikings' North Atlantic wanderings and Robin Hood's anti-aristocratic tendencies, the Marx company saw no reason not to fast-forward to American history, which was commemorated in its entirety by the plastic presidents in their dignified, Statuary Hall poses. More specific to American origins was a set of six 60-millimeter Revolutionary figures that included a drummer, fifer, and flag bearer copied from Archibald Willard's famous painting *The Spirit of 1776*; this set came with a hard plastic General Washington who was placed, quite literally, on a pedestal in the style of the presidents. The 54-millimeter Sons of Liberty playset, reissued as the Johnny Tremain set to tie in with the popular children's book and TV series, came complete with blue colonials, red redcoats, and six characters that included a lone woman named "Cilla," the colonial forebear of Mineral City's bonneted matron.

We've now arrived at the American frontier, represented by the 45-millimeter Fort Dearborn and the 54-millimeter Boonesborough and Alamo sets. Here, little Indians and Mexicans served as historical precursors to the Soviets: early opponents of American progress who resisted time's inevitable march toward one market under God, indivisible. That the Indians were indispensable icons of such resistance explains their otherwise unaccountable presence in the Alamo set. Nor does this set stress the fact that Davy Crockett and Colonel Travis were actually fighting for the Republic of Texas, thereby pursuing their own Indian-like opposition to the expanding United States. The goal of promoting American unity posed a special challenge when Marx issued a 1958 playset based on our most divisive struggle. Calling it the "Civil War" would have alienated southern buyers, but calling it the "War Between the States" would have puzzled everyone north of the Mason-Dixon line. The compromise, ingenious as well as descriptive of its figures, resulted in one Marx's best-selling playsets: the Blue and the Gray. The set was so popular that the Multiple Products Corporation issued a knockoff with a name that lay just this side of litigation: "The Blues and the Grays." The popularity of the Marx set hinged, in part, on the reassuring, above-the-fray demeanor of its character figures. Lincoln, Davis, Grant, and Lee appear as unaffected as Roy and Dale by violence that surrounds them; these stately heroes rendered the bloodiest conflict in American history safe for play.

This brings us to the Wild West, that endlessly reimagined site of contestation which Roy and Dale evoked but did not actually inhabit, although their Mineral City companions certainly did. Marx's most overt celebration of Manifest Destiny was a set of five western heroes: Daniel Boone, Davy Crockett, Kit Carson, General Custer, and, as if to demonstrate a winner's generosity, Sitting Bull. The western playsets, most notably Little Big Horn and the immensely popular Fort Apache, joined the frontier sets in exhibiting a crucial difference from Mineral City: red and yellow Indians provided the standard playset conflict between a clearly identifiable "us" and the "them" of a cultural and racial Other. For all its violence, however, Fort Apache contained less potential for playtime angst than the western town, which was populated solely by white Americans. The "injuns" caused the mayhem at Fort Apache, but at Mineral City we had only ourselves to blame.

In hindsight, Little Big Horn seems an odd choice for celebrating American history: didn't we lose that one? Still, the Little Big Horn set was fully consistent with a species of history that remembered by forgetting—or in this case, by undoing. Although a truly historical set would have positioned the Seventh Cavalry figures in various attitudes of rigor mortis, Marx's version brought Custer and his men to life again, itching for a do-over.

Apart from several World War II sets, Marx devoted only one historical playset that I know of to twentieth-century events: the Untouchables, a spinoff from another popular TV show. These 54-millimeter cops and gangsters, along with character figures of Eliot Ness and Al Capone, were members of our grandparents' generation. This fact makes it fortunate that I never owned the set: for whom would I have rooted? My grandmother, a card-carrying member of the Women's Christian Temperance Union, would have seen the feds as the good guys, as the set surely intended. But don't historical judgments always reflect who's doing the judging? When Grandma came to live with us, my father was forced to drink his beer out in the garage, and only at night. I loved Grandma, but my stronger loyalty to Dad would have prompted me to see Capone and the rum-runners as the good guys, with disastrous consequences. With everyone in the Untouchables set representing somebody's good guy, all play would have ground to a halt.

As our household division over the Eighteenth Amendment revealed, recent history is especially sensitive terrain, its conflicts too fresh in memory to be shrugged off. Although World War II was still a raw wound, I had a much easier time choosing sides among the soldiers than I would have had with the Untouchables. The aura of the Armed Forces Training Center was relatively peaceful, but in the various Battleground sets, which depicted Europe, Iwo Jima, and the Battle of the Rhine, the war became Fort Apache all over again. The Japanese and German soldiers looked like updated reincarnations of those troublesome Indians; their brutal expressions and antic poses made them easy to hate.

I find it astonishing to realize that I was playing with Marx soldiers and sailors only a little over a decade after Berlin, Hiroshima, and Nagasaki. We kids grasped, on some level, the terrifying recentness of the war: after all, the broad faces of our toy G.I.s, echoes of Bill Mauldin's wartime cartoons of Willie and Joe, were the faces of our own fathers. It was impossible not to make the connection, and thus see ourselves as winners — or at least, the sons of winners. The large object being dragged by a Training Center sailor looked exactly like the duffel bag in the back of our downstairs closet; the watch cap and dress whites stored in that bag were perfect matches with the little sailor's outfit.

This figure, in particular, reminded me that I was one lucky boy. If my father had not returned from the Navy, I would not be commanding his playset counterparts in tabletop campaigns. Indeed, I would never have been born.

Feeling lucky was common among postwar Americans, living as we were at the presumed apex of history. We kids learned from our playsets that history was a long and fitful prologue to now, a series of challenges that had to be overcome before people like us could finally evolve. Once upon a time there were cavemen, Romans, Indians, and a host of others who contributed, mostly negatively, to the story of how fifties America became possible. Proof of this narrative lay all around us: TV dinners, cars with aerodynamic fins, wonder drugs, and the promise of space travel. We ate better than Caesar, fought better than Sitting Bull, and behaved better than Tōjō. We kids were constantly told that we would live longer and grow up to be smarter than all the people who had gone before us. We were living at the "end of history," the catchy phrase that Johns Hopkins historian Francis Fukuyama, another fifties kid, would apply four decades later to an event for which we all yearned: the fall of the Soviet Union. I suspect that the young Fukuyama owned a Marx playset or two. Didn't these toys reinforce my generation's childhood belief that the final American equilibrium was at hand? Once we beat those troublesome Communists, as we surely would, everything would be perfect. This squared well with what we were learning about evolution in school: when a thing becomes perfect, whether it's a tree frog or a nation, there's no need for further change.

Deep down, the playsets issued at the midpoint of the American Century echoed the vision of Saint Augustine, whose *City of God* posited a linear movement toward divine perfection. This idea led twentieth-century paleontologist and priest Teilhard de Jardin to envision an entropic unity of spirit: at the end-time, all matter would diffuse into pure energy—into the One. Playset historiography also echoed, though more darkly, the Pax Romana embodied in the Ben Hur set: the mission to transform the Mediterranean Sea into a "Roman lake" reflected a similarly insistent reduction of diversity to unity. Drawing on inspiring and embarrassing precedents alike, Marx playsets embodied a progressivist theory of history that posited a gradual amelioration of all things, leading to their culmination in the American here and now.

Marx playset history was thus "Whig" history in the grand manner of Hippolyte Taine and Thomas Macaulay, both of whom shared Auguste Comte's positivism as well as the Enlightenment shift from God's city to the perfection of reason. Now it was rationality and science that propelled history down the path toward the America that these toys celebrated. Marx playsets, especially those based on TV shows and movies, also espoused Thomas Carlyle's "Great Man" view of history: Roy and Dale functioned as Mineral City's Great Man and Great Woman, with Pat Brady as Great Pal and Bullet as Great Dog. But the greatness did not stop there. Roy and Dale were not just buffers to Old West savagery, but touchstones for a child's very identity. The character figures in many playsets encouraged considerable self-satisfaction: children played with the nameless figures, but played *as* the named ones. This is the chief reason why little boys playing with Mineral City could feel good about themselves. If they wanted to walk the streets of Mineral City, Roy did the walking for them; ditto for little girls and Dale. The playset elevation of the child into a literal over-seer of a tiny community created a heady sense of control over time as well as space. When you strolled down Mineral City's tin-litho sidewalk in Roy's boots, you entered history not as its passive heir or helpless victim, but as its decisive agent: whatever went down in Mineral City, you were the one who made it happen.

While Mineral City fostered a teleological vision of history, its day-to-day workings were Hegelian to the core, an ongoing dialectic of cowboy conflict and resolution. The saloon could provide a ready-made stage for a Hegelian thesis: say, the peaceful figures lined up along the bar, hoisting beers and swapping yarns. This scene would eventually bore you, and you would find yourself saying something like "Uh oh! There's trouble!" At this point you would make the riding bandit knock down the harness-carrying man, rob the saloon, and leap on a horse to escape—and there was your antithesis. The adjusting forces of history reasserted themselves when you grabbed Sitting Roy and plunked him on Trigger to chase the bad guy down, which of course he always did. The full Hegelian synthesis came when the scofflaw had been put in jail and the harness-carrier was once again standing upright. This mini-crisis had moved history forward a little, because Standing Roy was now posted at the door to prevent further trouble. The macrocosmic trajectory of playset history, with its linear march toward perfection, was furthered by a cyclical process embodied in the endless enactment and reenactment of little stories like this one. Had Oswald Spengler and Arnold Toynbee visited Mineral City, they might have agreed that the outcome of bad-guy challenge and good-guy response was the reestablished order of a quiet Main Street.

Although the conflict-and-resolution plots central to historical playsets tempt me to say that Marx history was Marxist history, Louis Marx's devotion to free-market economics precludes that possibility. While playsets offered progress as a secular religion, safe returns from the past served as seductive opiates for the pint-sized masses. In addition, old-school Marxism holds that class struggle will eventually end in victory for the workers; in playset history, however, the elite Roy is still guarding the saloon. The deeper message of playset action was not a call for historical change, but an acceptance of how things were — or how they seemed, filtered through the corroborating lenses of commerce and the media. The real point was not to enter into the historical process, but to keep it at bay. Every time Roy whipped a Mineral City bad guy, the turmoil of the past had been overcome, once again, by a profoundly static present.

What were the underlying lessons of all this? The main one was that nothing was truly "historical" unless fighting was involved, a concession to the propensity of little boys — by nurture, nature, or both — to play rough. While countless playsets were based on wars and rumors of wars, playset history routinely ignored moments of accord. No Marx playset commemorated the Council of Nicea, the Treaty of Ghent, the Treaty of Versailles, the end of WWII, or the founding of the United Nations. A selective brand of historical memory also allowed playsets to sweep American embarrassments under the rug. The Marx presidents, for instance, were all posed with equal dignity whether they were Abraham Lincoln or Warren G. Harding. Had the presidential set been truly historical and not chiefly commemorative, the hard-plastic Harding might have been posed leaving his mistress's flat; William Henry Harrison, in office only a month before dying of pneumonia, might have been provided with a tiny plastic deathbed. In another example of playset-history absence, the Untouchables playset lacked its temporal companion: a Great Depression playset would surely have revealed the limits to which history can be sanitized. Finally, playsets shortchanged the processes of history, the complex interweavings of cause and effect. While the Marx Untouchables gamely tried to enforce Prohibition, there was no Temperance Movement playset—no 54-millimeter Baptists and Methodists not drinking—to show how one thing led to another. This static historiography reached all the way back to prehistory: although Marx's dinosaurs had to fight cavemen, they were spared the presence of the tiny proto-mammals that helped usher them out of the world.

As for grasping history's ever-problematic relation to "truth," we fifties kids never had a chance. We were receiving mutually reinforcing messages on so many fronts that it was impossible to separate reality from the buoyant representations of reality that bombarded us. When some of Marx's dinosaurs were reused in a Flintstones set, did their association with cartoon Fred and Barney make them less real? Roy and Dale were certainly real, but plenty of other playsets were based on TV shows that weren't: *Gunsmoke, Zorro, The Lone Ranger, Captain Gallant,* and so on. We kids knew, vaguely, that Wyatt Earp had been a real person, but what about Marshal Dillon and Miss Kitty? With all of them on TV and all of them rendered in plastic with equal detailing, fact and fiction kept blending into a cheerful muddle.

Of course, most children won't care if a story is true, so long as it's good. We kids arranged our figures and devised our stories blissfully unaware that we were following somebody else's master script. We *were* aware, on some level, of the playset assurance that we were history's winners, just like our fathers and our nation; indeed, this is why we loved these toys. As we devised little scenarios based on the Civil War, the Old West, or D-Day, we were absorbing what the American fifties embraced as history's great lesson: there's no time like the present.

And didn't tomorrow promise an even better present? The Indians were gone, but the Russians remained; once we beat them, we would go to outer space and beat whatever three-headed Indians or Russians awaited us there. The Marx company had the science-driven future covered in a variety of outer-space playsets: Cape Canaveral, Space Patrol, Rex Mars, the Tom Corbett Space Academy, and Operation Moon Base. The Corbett set included future Indians to fight in the guise of little aliens, several of whom packed guns and needed to be dealt with, Aggressive-Roy style. We kids were certain that beating them would be a small step for man: their defeat was the inevitable outcome of a story that we already knew by heart.

The feel-good lessons conveyed by these educational toys were powerful: like many fifties kids, I could have used some re-educational toys in my subsequent efforts to unlearn them. The real lesson of history is not that there's no time like the present, but that times change—and change permits insights that were formerly impossible to imagine. Seen in hindsight, the overarching story told by Marx's historical playsets was too predictable to be truly good. When a single Big Thing is calling the shots, whether it's God, Reason, or American Destiny, there's little room for surprise, only new steps toward a foregone conclusion. If everybody from Ben Hur gladiators to Battleground Nazis can be absorbed so effortlessly into a single master-plot, an excessively tidy narrative in which everything works out a little too well in the end, what suspense is possible?

The consequences of even a bad story, however, can outlive its telling—and in my case, the chief consequence is guilt. I waged horrific wars with my Battleground G.I.s in the empty lot next door, knocking down rows of army men with tennis balls, bombing Jeeps and tanks with dirt clods, and even setting fire to a plastic Nazi or two. I'm tempted to invoke the standard "boys will be boys" excuse for such childhood savagery; the persistent aggression of males throughout history might even lend it some validity. But I cannot let myself off the hook. How can I, when I can still recall the bad-boy smell of burning plastic as I gleefully watched tiny Germans warp beyond recognition? I can't let Louis Marx off the hook, either. Didn't he make the faces of those Nazi soldiers so repulsive that they seemed to beg for some lighter fluid and a match?

But here's a more immediate question: wouldn't it be a shame if this desktop crowd, collected at considerable expenditure of time and money, ended up making me feel bad? After all, it's not the fault of playset figures that they told bad stories. Then, too, I seriously doubt that I would have been a kinder, gentler boy in their absence. Although time has exposed the deeply flawed ideology embodied in these objects, the Toy King and I did not share a pathological love of violence so much as a failure of imagination—and failures of imagination are rarely willful. The cultural scripts that we followed did not allow for much wiggle room: Marx could not imagine not making those soldiers, and I could not imagine not burning them up.

The limits that these old toys once placed on my imagination surely explain my compulsion to play differently with them today. Maybe they can redeem their unsavory historical legacy by helping to dissolve any vestigial power of their original stories. Maybe I can redeem my childhood arrogance in absorbing those stories and thinking that I, too, was above the historical fray. The silly grin on Friar Tuck's face reminds me of all the airy notions that I once entertained and all the complex realities that I never grasped. Tuck acquired his grin in the mold—and though he can't wipe it off, perhaps he can learn to smile for new reasons that have nothing to do with the old playset agon of us versus them, good guys versus bad.

Tuck's jovial expression also reminds me that I need to lighten up a bit. Maybe I'm still taking the "educational" claims of historical playsets too seriously. These were not textbooks, after all, but toys, and their historical distortions are roughly equivalent to the lack of philosophical discourse in a Burt Reynolds movie: is either worth ranting about? And isn't a critique that benefits from a half-century's hindsight a little too easy? Such grumbling would in fact reflect the classic baby boomer mistake of prolonging the smugness that we absorbed from childhoods swaddled in postwar feelings of superiority. I don't wish to repeat the mistakes that I made as a ten-year-old. The past even the relatively recent past—really *is* another country, and to condemn old toys for their political incorrectness would be to assert, yet again, the superiority of the present.

Besides, hasn't history always reflected the limits of somebody's imagination? History marshals facts into a coherent story—and a story inevitably articulates the storyteller's dream. Herodotus, the "Father of History," had a dream about the normative status of Greek culture as opposed to the "exotic" lands that he visited. Livy dreamed that Rome had always been destined to rule the world. The people who wrote my schoolbooks had a similar dream about America, and so did Louis Marx. Playset history merely reiterated age-old ways of imagining the past. After Aristotle famously claimed that poetry was more useful than history because it expressed elevating ideals rather than dull realities, ancient historians tried to prove him wrong by promoting some ideals of their own. Livy was typical in seeing history as a vehicle for individual and communal improvement, a ready source of moral lessons. Plutarch recounted the lives of his "noble" Greeks and Romans so that readers could learn from their example and thereby live more virtuously. If history always yields the lessons that the historian is seeking, we shouldn't be surprised when its lessons change with the seekers. Herodotus divided the world into Greeks and "barbarians"; Louis Marx divided the world into Americans and everyone else.

Although Marx passed along this dichotomy, unchallenged and unaltered, to the younger me who played with his toys, at least I got to play with them. For all their political incorrectness, Marx playsets performed one unambiguous act of social good: they democratized the toy industry. Mass-produced and inexpensively priced, these items were sold by Sears and at dime stores to kids who were definitely not rich. Playset figures were not handmade items crafted from metal or wood in the German tradition of Marx's old employer, Ferdinand Strauss, but bits of cheap plastic, products of an emerging everyman technology called injection molding. In its rush to celebrate contemporary America, Mineral City clearly glossed over the more problematic issues surrounding the "taming" of the Old West: the displacement of the Indians, the ambient violence, the abuse of natural resources. And yet, it authentically embodied the American ideals of democracy and prosperity in its very existence as a cheaply produced assemblage of vinyl people, plastic accessories, and sheets of lithographed tin. We're not talking F.A.O. Schwarz here: when my parents bought Mineral City, they paid all of $5.89, the same price as my Armed Forces Training Center. The Alamo and Cape Canaveral sets sold for $5.98; the Blue and the Gray, $7.88. The 196-piece Fort Apache and the lavish Ben Hur set, impressive even in its smaller, 130-piece version, were both available at Sears for $7.98. And as late as 1963, the two sizes of the Iwo Jima Battleground cost only $4.44 and $9.44. Although Louis Marx may have been a jingoistic American and an unrepentant capitalist, he was no hypocrite. This Henry Ford of the toy industry got rich by bringing a better life—or at least better toys—to thousands of lower- and middle-class American kids.

Then again, how likely is it that Louis Marx had social and economic reform in mind when he priced his toys so cheaply? I seem to want it both ways. I'd like a grown-up excuse for playing with these toys, but I don't wish to idealize the "good old days" in which I first encountered them. In the end, playset history confirms the same truth as real-world history: times change—and sometimes they change a lot. The past five decades have made painfully clear the historical arrogance and unreflective nationalism of Marx playsets. But while the playsets themselves cannot be rehabilitated, it seems possible to redeem the plastic figures that came with them. If these little people can be detached from the Big Story that they originally told, maybe they can tell better stories that can be embraced and inhabited now.

The possibility of this lies in the simple fact that everyone in the desktop crowd—good guys and bad guys, character figures and also-rans—stands side by side, their arrangement random to the point of thematic illegibility. Blissfully de-narratized, these figures are no longer telling any Big Story: they aren't winning the West or beating the Huns or doing much of anything, really, except gazing at the Standing Roy who addresses them from the top of that barrel. Although their current arrangement pleases me, countless smaller scenes have been equally satisfying: an Auburn Rubber pioneer and a Marx Nativity wise man conversing with a vinyl G.I. and the Mineral City matron; the Bar-M Ranch guitar-playing cowboy serenading a reclining Cleopatra made by Cherilea of England; the Marx farm wife dancing with Friar Tuck, whose smile now seems far more innocent. I have placed the Marx Jesus and Louis Marx himself, nicely matched in 60-millimeter hard plastic, face to face so that they can exchange their views of history in a playset world that, for once, has no history.

The flawed historical vision of Mineral City can be nullified once its citizens have been recast in different roles. I can attest, from first-hand experience, that the playset past can be rewritten—or perhaps more accurately, unwritten—by rescuing these figures from their old narrative rigidities. When you put the two-pistoled sheriff next to a recast Richard Nixon, stiff in his ill-fitting suit, you're no longer anticipating a fight; instead, you're observing two attendees at an antique gun show. When you see the elegant Marx dollhouse father, crisply suited and holding a pipe, chatting with several Marx and Auburn road workers, you're witnessing a reconciliation of socioeconomic classes. When you place the Marx Jesus in amicable conversation with two Captain Gallant Arabs and a Nativity wise man, a story of ecumenical peace assumes tangible form before your eyes.

Such unexpected juxtapositions serve to destabilize the tightly-knit plots that once animated these figures. There's no historical progress here, just a bunch of little people entering into endlessly shifting realignments, like atoms combining and recombining into different molecules. Reimagined as part of an ongoing conversation that can be invented and reinvented at will, these figures are ironically confirming that there really *is* no time like the present—especially the present of this desktop. Here there is no past and future, cause and effect, origin and legacy, conflict and resolution, or anger and reprisal. There is no sense of what might have been, should have been, or has to be—no mantle of greatness or shame falling from one pair of shoulders onto another. Maybe this is what the real end of history will look like. As I gaze at this motley crowd, I am recovering something of that dream-like escape from the grip of time and place that I enjoyed when I played with some of these figures as a child. This time around, however, there are no winners or losers, no good guys or bad. There are only 150 or so little people from all sorts of times and places, huddled together and listening in rapt attention as Roy tells them a brand-new story that I would give anything to hear.

Little Big World

n the third row of the desktop crowd stands a 60-millimeter Hubert Humphrey, the only person represented by the thousand-some playset figures in my collection whom I actually met in the flesh. The encounter took place in 1961, during a family vacation to Washington, D.C. One day, while my father and sister were visiting the natural history museum, my mother took me to the Capitol. When Mom, a liberal Democrat and longtime fan, called Humphrey's office and asked if she could meet him, the senior senator from Minnesota graciously came to the Senate Reception Room for a brief chat. I remember shaking his hand and thinking that he was much taller than he looked in pictures. I must have blurted out something like "I'm a Democrat, too!" because I also remember him bending down and saying, "Good for you!"

If the incident proved anything, it was that neither Hubert Humphrey nor the eleven-year-old me possessed a shred of psychic ability. If we had, we might have shared the chilling recognition that almost half a century later, when he was thirty years dead, a plastic version of him would be standing on my desk. The Marx company produced this figure seven years after our encounter, when Humphrey was serving as Lyndon Johnson's vice president and starting his own bid for the presidency. Around this time I had a second sighting when Humphrey spoke at my college. I was a percussionist in the band, and as we were playing him to the podium with a fanfare, I muffed a cymbal crash. I have always regretted this mishap: was the pathetic click produced by the air pocket in those cymbals an omen of what Nixon would do to "the Happy Warrior" in the coming election?

Despite his upbeat nickname, Hubert Humphrey knew disappointment. So does his 60-millimeter counterpart: if it weren't for the "Mar-X" logo on the bottom of the base, you would never guess that this is a genuine Marx figure. The waxy plastic and vague detailing, a sad fall from the toy presidents that it imitated, betray the general decline in the quality of Marx products during the late sixties. My figure, factory painted in glossy colors, arrived in its original bag with a header card that identified it simply as "H. Humphrey." "Made in Hong Kong" appeared on one side of the card; "Made for Pretested Promotions, Inc., New York, New York" on the other. Most collectors identify this figure as a production error, claiming that the company anticipated Humphrey's election and issued it to update their presidents set. This seems likely: for one thing, there are a lot of Marx Humphreys afoot (mine cost only three dollars); for another, the header card shows the number thirty-seven, which would have been his presidential order. On some of these figures, the back of the base reads "1969–": the starting date of an administration that never was.

Maybe it wasn't my inept cymbal crash that jinxed the Happy Warrior, but instead his premature rush into plastic. When I removed the paint with rubbing alcohol and saw the figure's washed-out, indistinct features, the Marx Humphrey was exposed for what it was: a sign of the end-times, of doing things on the cheap. If I had actually *been* psychic on that day in the Capitol, I would have pulled the senator down to my level and whispered solemnly in his ear: "Don't ever let anyone make you into a toy."

Marx playsets had two chief selling points. The first was that they were "realistic," a claim that I accepted completely as a child. I was confident that my Mineral City playset would make me feel perfectly at home if I ever visited the real West, wherever that was. I was equally certain that my Armed Forces Training Center and Battleground set accurately showed what joining the army and fighting a war would be like. The pictures in my brother's American history textbook also proved that the Marx presidents were faithful copies of their flesh-and-blood counterparts.

Marx's second claim was that these miniature worlds helped prepare children for the big world—but here, my toys seemed to fall short. Tiny presidents, cowboys, and soldiers offered scant preparation for the grown-up life that I seemed destined to live. The absence of real-life cowboys in our small town rendered Roy and Dale's West impossibly remote. My future as a soldier—a future that every Cold

War boy presumed—lay too far off for my army men to yield any immediate lessons. And how likely was it that I would ever see George Washington or Woodrow Wilson strolling down Main Street or sipping coffee in Wilson's sandwich shop? Marx made plenty of playsets that portrayed everyday life: service stations, skyscrapers, airports, department stores, and so on. Although these playsets might have offered some real-world preparation, I owned none of them. Any fifties boy who fretted over how he would do as an adult would have reached the same conclusion that I did: I had the wrong toys.

What I yearned for was playset versions of everyday people. Little soldiers, cowboys, and presidents were fine, but little teachers, policemen, and store clerks might have spoken more directly to the central question of my childhood: what was it like to be a grown-up? Curious but painfully shy, I assumed that I could learn about real adults by studying toy adults, but with no risk of getting yelled at for staring. The curiosity came from my mother, whose favorite pastime was what she called "people watching." She practiced this hobby with a boldness that I envied but could not emulate, owing to the shyness that I had inherited from my father, an eyes-straight-ahead sort of man whose chief goal was to get through the day unnoticed. When it came to social ease, these two were flat opposites; my brother, sister, and I sometimes wondered how they had ever gotten together. Mom often seemed lost in thought as she watched Dad reading the newspaper, which he always held in front of his face.

Other grown-ups were even more baffling. I could tell, from watching them going about their mysterious business, that there was a lot to learn before I could navigate the big world of Findlay, Ohio. Indeed, the town seemed filled with secrets. A neighborhood man who tended bar was rumored to be "seeing" another woman—but didn't I see other people every day? A body was once fished out of the Blanchard River, but by the time we kids arrived at the scene, there was nothing to see except our own reflections staring back from beneath the Blanchard Street bridge. The mysterious "hoboes" who camped out in the nearby fairgrounds sometimes came to our back door for handouts; Mom made them sandwiches, but wouldn't let me talk to them. I knew from my father that the Republicans were "out to get the working man," but I bent this pronouncement to a child's understanding and kept trying, without success, to catch a Republican beating somebody up. Even public events seemed to contain secrets. The town's sesquicentennial, the largest civic celebration of my childhood, boiled down to collecting "Fort Findlay" coins that were good for car washes and specials on dry cleaning. Everybody seemed excited anyway: what was I missing?

Only the infrequent disasters were what they appeared to be. The deeper significance of tornadoes was perfectly clear from the splintered barns and bloated cow carcasses that they left behind; whenever our family rushed to the basement in response to a storm siren, I knew exactly what was going on. When a spring flood cut off Findlay's east side and my older brother and I rode to the A&P in an army truck to buy food, the trip was exciting but not at all mysterious. One day, the YMCA caught fire; my most vivid memory, however, is not the orange glow that filled the early evening sky, but the creepy excitement on my sister's face when she rushed into the house with the news: "Hey, did you hear? The Y's burning down!" I felt that same expression spreading across my face as I hopped on my bike and raced downtown to watch the spectacle. At last, something was happening.

The YMCA fire stands out against an indistinct backdrop that was far more typical of a child's life in Findlay: a vignette in which we neighborhood kids are just standing around, waiting for something to happen. Convinced that there had to be more going on than what we could see, we felt shut out of all sorts of interesting things, though we couldn't imagine what they might be. When would we get to experience the excitement that grown-ups surely felt every day?

Lacking toys with which to break through our town's tranquil surface, I made do by putting the toys that I did own to unintended uses. My plastic presidents, for instance, could be reimagined as regular Findlay people: nicely dressed civilians who mingled with soldiers, cowboys, and dinosaurs in mini-dramas that had nothing to do with the American past, but everything to do with the small-town present. My favorites for this purpose were not the most famous presidents, but the ones who most resembled the people whom I saw every day. Washington and Lincoln rarely left the box: too recognizable *as* Washington and Lincoln, they lacked the versatility necessary for this kind of play. With their business suits, the twentieth-century presidents were the best stand-ins for regular people—along with Zachary Taylor, in his modern-looking double-breasted coat. In a pinch, the

Gilded Age crowd could also serve as regular people: with their formal coats and full beards, they could be celebrating the sesquicentennial.

Although I was eager to grant one Marx president his real-life political role, I didn't own him because my set ended with Eisenhower. Given our family's politics, this fact irritated me; after Kennedy's election I kept checking the dime stores for a plastic JFK to celebrate the happy days that were surely here again. Although the Marx company indeed updated its set with a Kennedy figure, I never found one—and a bit of historical hindsight suggests why. In the 1960 election, Hancock County cast 17,059 votes for Nixon and only 6,712 for Kennedy: why would the local merchants rub salt in all those Republican wounds by filling their toy bins with exultant little JFKs? At the time, of course, this explanation eluded me. Confident that a Marx Kennedy would turn up sooner or later, I bided my time.

The Eisenhower foursome—two poses of Ike and two of Mamie—were the very best stand-ins for ordinary grown-ups among the presidential figures: they looked like the people whom I saw at church, the post office, and the bank. I liked Ike, as most everyone did in the fifties, but a boy-Democrat will naturally prefer him in plastic. While my soldiers, cowboys, and dinosaurs offered ample escape into places that I didn't know, my Ikes and Mamies whetted a growing appetite for toys that might shed some light on the place where I actually lived. On this score, the Eisenhowers were realistic with a vengeance: after all, they were Republicans.

The recent presidents were soon joined in the role of regular people by my favorite army men, a select group of some twenty culled from over a hundred. I called this group the Keepers. A mix of Marx and Auburn Rubber 60-millimeter G.I.s, the figures were for the most part not shooting guns or throwing hand grenades, but just standing around. With their individualized faces and vaguely familiar poses, the Keepers rivaled Ravishing Dale and the Marx dinosaurs as my most cherished toys. I never risked deploying these soldiers in dirt clod wars with friends, as I did with my other army men. Instead, I reserved them for solitary excursions into a realm that I was both eager and scared to enter: the big world where things actually happened. My favorite Keepers were a Marx G.I. lugging a suitcase and two Auburn soldiers who appeared to be taking a break. My father told me that the suitcase guy was carrying ammunition, but this soldier could also be an encyclopedia salesman or Fuller Brush man peddling wares at a construction site. Clearly, the two soldiers on break were lookers rather than doers: one was pointing at something while the other puffed on a cigarette, waiting for something to happen.

An elite corps of everyday grown-ups, the Keepers tested miniature bomb shelters dug out of hillsides and enjoyed the space-age amenities of solar houses built from discarded bricks and windowpanes. They enacted endless baseball games, with plays determined either by dice or by my own godlike fiat. When I read *Huckleberry Finn*, they took leisurely cruises down Lye Creek in a soap dish, and after I finished a children's version of *The Iliad*, they reenacted scenes — somewhat hammily — from the Trojan War. Bravely assuming their deeper identities not as soldiers but as regular people exploring a giant realm, they inched across the linoleum counter toward the Giant Cookie Jar in the Giant Kitchen. They tested their balance on the Giant Turntable, managing fairly well at 33⅓ RPMs but faltering badly at 45. None could withstand the Whirlpool of Death, which spun at 78, unless they were taped down. The Keepers also patiently served as artist's models when I was learning to draw people. A few of them, weighted with fishing sinkers, soared into the sky and "floated" back to earth — always a little too quickly — in handkerchief parachutes.

One terrible day, a playmate threw one of the Keepers into a field of tall weeds at the fairgrounds, where we were building an Amazonian greenhouse city out of discarded pop bottles and canning jars. After searching on hands and knees until it grew too dark to see, I was unable to explain to my parents why losing a lump of plastic made me miss dinner. How could they possibly understand my guilt at letting this army man down? It didn't help that he was the most worried-looking Keeper — the worst man, certainly, to end up alone in the uncharted Brazilian jungle that stretched between the sheep barn and the grandstand. I returned to the spot for weeks, but never found him. Nor would I see his anxious face again until I opened an eBay box half a century later.

The English professor in me would say that by making these soldiers serve as everything *but* soldiers, I was constantly decontextualizing them, just as I am doing now with the figures on this desktop. Maybe my current way of playing with these old toys — this obsession with new and improved playset stories—is not an innovation after all, but a revived memory. Don't I recall discovering that Roy and Dale could also serve as regular people once I removed them from Mineral City and let them mingle with the Keepers and the modern-looking presidents? Standing Roy fit the everyman role quite well: he wore the noncommittal expression of the adult midwestern male that I was expected to become. Except for the lost army man, the Keepers had that look, too—and so did my father, whose face in repose conveyed a bland stoicism that made him look ready for anything. If I learned how to control my features like that, maybe my grown-up face would be properly noncommittal, another necessary step for moving out into the big world. The presidents also helped out. Although Taft, Wilson, and FDR were too jovial for this purpose, the others looked appropriately serious, not like the rabbity boy that I was trying hard not to be.

The Keepers and their auxiliaries kept raising a persistent boyhood question: how did adults manage to get along so peacefully, when we kids got into fights almost every day? What was it that kept grown-ups from constantly beating each other up? I probed this mystery by putting my regular-people figures together and watching them not fight. Amity prevailed, though I wasn't sure why, whenever Teddy Roosevelt chatted at length with the smoking Keeper, or whenever a barbershop quartet consisting of Taft, Coolidge, Hoover, and Truman serenaded Ravishing Dale. Placing these figures into random arrangements and chance conversations made the grown-up realm seem less intimidating. The fact that nobody in my little world seemed concerned about getting beaten up made the big world seem like a place where I might do all right after all.

Standing before me now are more—and more varied—playset guides to adult life than I ever dreamed of owning as a child. Some of these figures might have eased my fears as I began venturing out into the big world beyond our neighborhood. Most of them possess that fifties adult male face, with its inscrutable mix of purpose and calm. They seem to know exactly who they are, just as the grown-ups in our town seemed to know exactly who they were.

The farmers, whether by Marx, Auburn Rubber, or Ohio Art, display the noble, Grant Wood frontality of people of the land. These pleasant-faced figures contradict my father's advice never to become a farmer because the work is hard and endless. Dad knew this first-hand: in his only extant boyhood picture, he is definitely not smiling like the Marx farm lad. The Marx Happi-Time and Lazy-Day farm playsets, had I owned them, would have struck my father as laughable misnomers, playtime denials of the isolation and drudgery that drove him off his parents' small farm in downstate Illinois at the earliest opportunity. He didn't need "gay Paree" to resist staying down on the farm; all it took was Terre Haute. Dad escaped to a post office, to a tank farm, to the navy, and back to a tank farm. He made his final escape after he took some correspondence courses in accounting and wound up in what was, for him, an uncomfortably quiet office.

My father's transformation from blue collar to white confused me: I had no idea what an "accountant" did for a living. It was easier to understand his old job on the tank farm, relics of which were still in our basement: a hardhat, an assortment of coveralls and boots, and a sizable collection of tools. Although several early-era Dads are standing on my desk, the Marx construction workers look less happy than my father does in photographs taken when he worked as a pipeliner and electrician for the Ohio Oil Company, which later became Marathon Oil. Closer playset parallels to the open face in my father's tank-farm photos come from the Auburn Rubber Company, whose civilian workers clearly reflect the fifties idealization of American labor. Basking in the glow of postwar productivity, some of these workers are even wearing faint smiles. Like the men in Thomas Hart Benton paintings or murals found in union halls, these railroad workers, gas station attendants, utility workers, policemen, and firemen are ruggedly handsome: all share a resemblance to Bert Parks, except for an overweight cop who looks like Alfred Hitchcock. One of the Auburn utility men, his work-belt containing a looped cable and a large wrench, could serve as a reasonably accurate avatar for my tank-farm father.

Sadly, I've yet to find a playset accountant. Indeed, not many vintage playset figures depict my father's later working life as a regular person dressed for the office. Some of the modern presidents come close, but Ike was Ike and Truman was Truman: neither could be my father—though the latter, as a fellow midwestern Democrat, offers the more acceptable stand-in. Other potential Accountant Dads include the Marx Pet Shop father and the two Marx Dollhouse fathers, but these figures look far more at ease in their coats and ties than my father ever did. The Marx Untouchables set offers additional possibilities; the outfits are right, but the machine guns are a little off. The closest parallels to my office-worker Dad and his regular-people colleagues can be found in the Marx Skyscraper set. This seems fitting: Findlay's sole approximation of a skyscraper was the eight-storey Marathon Oil building, where my father refashioned himself from a *Honeymooners* dad into a *Father Knows Best* dad, though one who couldn't wait to shed his coat and tie when he got home. Whenever my father took me to the office, an eerily quiet place that reminded me of school during a test, I saw flesh-and-blood prototypes of several Skyscraper figures: the secretary, the two men with briefcases, the balding boss who holds a piece of paper.

It seems ironic that the Skyscraper set, with its New York City ambience, would offer the most accurate playset representation available of the workings of small-town Ohio—especially since the Skyscaper figures now fetch New York rather than Ohio prices. Though I know most of these figures only from photos on eBay listings, the pictures confirm that the set included regular Findlay people beyond my father's office colleagues. I often saw the Skyscraper woman with a toddler at the A&P. The Skyscraper pharmacist is a fair approximation, in uniform though not in face, of Mr. Shoemaker at B&G Drugs. In a pinch, the Skyscraper newsboy could be a thicker, cheerier version of my older brother, although Dave delivered his papers from a bike rather than hawking them on a street corner. The Skyscraper Ping-Pong players could be seen at Findlay's Teen Center, where my sister Sue hung out. And didn't I confront the flesh-and-blood prototype of the no-nonsense Skyscraper gym coach in junior high, where I got Cs in Phys Ed for not trying hard enough? The set even included a bank customer filling out a deposit slip. This figure, had I owned it as a child, could have relieved the Eisenhowers as they stood in line to deposit their fat Republican paychecks.

Most of Marx's everyday-life playsets, however, would have done little to ease my transition into the big world. The Sears Store playset would only have puzzled me. Sears was where Mom took us to buy school clothes: why play at something that you hate doing in real life? The Little Red Schoolhouse would also have left me cold. With its goody-two-shoes children and point-making teacher, I could only have replayed those boring, real-life schooldays in which nobody got spanked and nothing much happened. The Boy Scout Camp might actually have frightened me: certain that I would prove inept at tying knots and building fires, I avoided the Scouts despite my mother's conviction that joining might prevent me from becoming as antisocial as my father. There were also a few playset guides to the mysterious realm of girls and dating, which I knew was coming. Although I received some preparation for this in my longstanding crush on Ravishing Dale, I'm grateful that I never saw the Marx bathing beauties or the Marx campus cuties. Catlike and leering, these plastic pinups would have made me run to the nearest monastery, had I known what a monastery was and what people never did there.

Still, I can't help lamenting some playset absences, both then and now. Although I've found a good stand-in for my early-career father in the Auburn lineman, this desktop still lacks a satisfactory Accountant Dad. Sadly, there's no playset English professor here, either. But what is life in the big world if not an ongoing process of making do? Rather than standing around and waiting for a 60-millimeter professor to turn up, I've joined the crowd anyway, in the form of a figure from the Marx Jesus and the Apostles set. Bearded, balding, and middle-aged, Simon the Zealot stands among his desktop companions wearing a decidedly un-zealous expression. He looks sleepy and perhaps confused; my compulsion to identify with him suggests that after all these years, I'm still waiting for something to happen. Until it does, I am content to let this obscure apostle serve as my plastic backup, my personal *ushabti* figure. It's a relief to know that if I were to remove my glasses and don a bathrobe, I would exist here at two scales: sixty millimeters and five feet ten. And while Simon is not a perfect match, I'm grateful for the approximation: it would be a shame to be present on my own desktop only as an absence.

Playset figures seem to have acquired the opposite role from the one that they played in my childhood. Then, they helped a boy imagine his future; now, they're letting a grown-up reimagine his past. Some of these figures represent real people from that past. A few of them— Roy, Dale, Pat Brady, Jackie Gleason—were mainstays of fifties television; others, like Eisenhower and Humphrey, were prominent in fifties politics. I remember these people vividly: they seemed so powerful and accomplished that it was impossible to believe that they had once been children. Now the roles have reversed. Their playset counterparts have become the children, and I'm the grown-up who has been charged with arranging them, dusting them off, and checking periodically to see if anyone has fallen over.

Some of the real people standing here played decisive roles in a YMCA-fire-scale event that made the little world of our family seem perfectly in tune, for once, with the big world of America. I spent the evening of the 1960 election lying on the floor in front of the TV, moving army men into Democratic piles and Republican piles as the returns came in. Although we kids went to bed before the California results were announced, everyone woke up excited: after eight years of Republican rule, Jack Kennedy had finally snatched the presidency away from what my father called the "party of the rich." Dad found it especially sweet that JFK had beaten the worst Republican of all, "that bastard Nixon." My father's joy reminded me of an incident two years earlier, when he and I were watching a TV news report about Vice President Nixon's trip to Venezuela. As an angry mob began swarming around Nixon's car, Dad waved a bottle of beer at the screen and yelled, "*Get* the sonovabitch!" Such anger was perhaps understandable in a man who had spent his entire life in small midwestern towns, surrounded by Republicans who saw his hero FDR as the devil incarnate. At the time, though, his outburst puzzled me: wasn't that *our* vice president getting mobbed?

Although Nixon made it out of Caracas in one piece, my father got his revenge at Kennedy's election. Our family couldn't know, of course, how short-lived those happy days would be. While we were all watching the Kennedy funeral and listening to that spooky cadence of muffled drums, I got out my Marx presidents to witness the passing of one of their own. As I was lining up the figures, it occurred to me—probably for the first time in my life—that something I had wished for would never come true: I would never get a Marx JFK. I knew that even if I found one, buying it would only make me sad. After the funeral I carefully packed my presidents away; I don't recall ever playing with them again.

But as the saying goes, never say never. Around three years ago I finally acquired a Marx JFK and Jackie, thereby filling a collector's gap that ran deeper than most. Actually seeing and touching these figures brought a mild chill, along with an odd feeling that seemingly inalterable stories from the big world can somehow be rewritten in the little world of this desktop. A month later I bought a second pair of Kennedys: now I had one First Couple for the desktop crowd and another for safekeeping with the other presidents in an original box. Soon afterward, as if to overcompensate for a boyhood deprived of Camelot in plastic, I bought a third JFK. The three Marx Kennedys are not identical. Two are the final versions: gleaming white like the other presidents, they have Kennedy's presidential order—35th—molded on the back of their bases. The third is an off-white "candidate" figure, with slightly coarser features and an awkwardly positioned arm. The candidate figure, in particular, reinforces this eerie sense that old toys can somehow alter time and avert sad outcomes. The inscription on its base records a birth but not yet a death: "1917–."

The plastic versions of flesh-and-blood people give the desktop crowd an inescapable poignancy. The 60-millimeter Hubert Humphrey seems especially dismissive of the barriers that separate past from present and little world from big: didn't I once shake hands with this figure's living prototype? My father would be doubly convinced that all sorts of categories are getting blurred here, because he saw two of these real people.

One was my old bank customer. Several months after V-E Day, when Eisenhower was scheduled to review the troops at Newport, Rhode Island, my father and my Uncle Haven, who were both in the Navy, hitchhiked down from Charlestown to pay their respects to the Allied supreme commander. Unable to find a good vantage point, they climbed a lamppost opposite the reviewing stand. For over half an hour, as a cold wind whipped through their peacoats and company after company passed beneath Ike's gaze, the brothers clung to the pole and directed a steady salute toward the general. When they finally caught his eye, Ike flashed his crooked grin and snapped them a return salute. Whenever my father told this story, he insisted that he wouldn't have held that salute for so long if he had known that Eisenhower would someday run for president as a Republican. As a general, though, Ike was all right: didn't he take the trouble to acknowledge a couple of enlisted men?

The second real person in this crowd whom Dad encountered was responsible for that glaring absence in my Marx presidents. During those navy years, Uncle Haven became friends with fellow sailor Robert Kennedy, who invited my uncle and my father to dinner one night at the home of John Francis "Honey Fitz" Fitzgerald, Bobby's grandfather and the former mayor of Boston. There they met the young Jack, who was gearing up for his first political campaign: a run for the House of Representatives. In the course of the evening, my father-to-be and the president-to-be sat on a piano bench and chatted privately for about half an hour. Years later, during JFK's presidency, we kids pumped Dad for details of the big night, but he couldn't recall much except that the Kennedys had been nice, just like regular people. As he put it, they had "carried themselves well."

Kennedy and Eisenhower also carry themselves well in this desktop world. Ike is here as a Marx general rather than a Marx president: this figure, whom my father would doubtless call the "good" Ike, stands next to my old conversation partner, Hubert Humphrey. Nearby, Jack Kennedy has been reunited with Jackie, who is as beautiful as I remember even though she's a little big-faced, like Ravishing Dale. I consider it a minor miracle that this hard-plastic Jackie has survived unscathed for nearly half a century; her tiny ankles look alarmingly snappable.

Two rows behind the Kennedys stands a recast Marx Nixon, his dour presence reflecting a prevailing impulse, at this stage of my life, to let bygones be bygones. Not far from Nixon is a bright orange Auburn Rubber lineman, who could be—and at this moment is—my father before he traded his coveralls for a coat and tie. I don't think that Dad would mind having his playset avatar standing so close to Nixon. For one thing, a recast Jackie Gleason in his Ralph Kramden role is standing between them—and wasn't *The Honeymooners* one of Dad's favorite shows? For another, my father's hatred of Republicans mellowed as he aged, especially after he enjoyed a second vindication by outliving his old nemesis. When Nixon died, Dad generously promoted him to "that poor bastard."

A little over two years ago, my father, a month shy of his ninetieth birthday, joined Nixon and the rest of this crowd in the endless caravan that carries us all out of the big world. Dad declined rapidly in his final months, and on a visit to Columbus for what would be his last Thanksgiving, I tried to cheer him up—and perhaps redeem a collector's excess—by presenting him with one of my Marx Kennedys.

Peering closely at the figure's face, Dad gave a final retelling of the familiar story about a memorable night, once upon a time in Boston. Then he hoisted the figure aloft and proclaimed, "Jack was a good man."

I'd say that a couple of good men chatted that night in Boston. Thanks to the time-bending power of old toys, two navy veterans and lifelong Democrats are sharing time and space, once again, in the little big world of my desktop. My father has just switched avatars for the occasion: from the Auburn lineman to a 70-millimeter Ideal sailor. As I arrange the sailor and a Marx Kennedy to face each other, it is easy to imagine that a sixty-five-year-old conversation between a pipeliner who became an accountant and a congressman who became a president has not yet ended, not really. And why should it? They seem to be having a perfectly good time.

Left-Handed Jesus ....

W henever a box of old playset figures arrives in the mail, I stage a desktop ceremony. After lining up the new arrivals to face the crowd, I gather a permanent welcoming committee of four: Standing Roy, Al the allosaurus, an original figure of Louis Marx, and a Marx Jesus from the apostles set. After the first three offer imagined greetings, the Marx Jesus blesses each new arrival with a tap on the head; figures with warped feet or damaged bases occasionally swoon and fall under his hardplastic touch. Following the ceremony I return Jesus to his usual position at the back of the crowd, where he resumes an ongoing conversation with a second Louis Marx, this one a recast from the 1990s. After placing a few choice arrivals among the figures on my desk, I sort the rest into plastic bags.

In the smaller world as in the larger, ritual is a reaffirmation of order: it performs a realigning of all things in their proper places, like those figures in their bags. The welcoming ritual began several months ago when I idly performed it at the arrival of some Auburn Rubber G.I.s: the fact that it felt deeply right prompted an irresistible conviction that it had to continue or some sort of code would be violated. I imagine that the prevalent response to the ceremony among its desktop participants is gratitude for beating the odds by avoiding loss or destruction: their presence here reminds them of thousands of absent peers. For the collector who cannot resist projecting such emotions onto these objects, the welcoming ceremony evokes a time when bedtime prayers had to be said just right and Mom's health demanded that sidewalk cracks be avoided at all cost. I suspect that I've kept Roy, Al, Louis, and Jesus so busy because rituals create realities—and realities, once created, can be ignored only at considerable risk. Some things simply have to be done, and done right.

Religion in 1950s America had a spooky urgency to it. Although this was partly a backlash against the cheerful commercialism that followed World War II, it was also a response to the looming presence of the bomb in our national consciousness. Everyone shared the nagging expectation that despite the better life promised by new housing developments, household conveniences, and the polio vaccine, any given day might bring the rise of a mushroom cloud over the nearest big city. Children process ambient fear in oddly particularized ways: I remember worrying that the animals at the Toledo Zoo, fifty miles to the north, would be caught defenseless in their cages when the bomb went off. You didn't have to be an anxious child to harbor dark thoughts like this. Despite the booming economy and the rampant consumerism encouraged by the still-new medium of television, the scary rhetoric of the Cold War was everywhere.

Not even Roy and Dale singing "Happy Trails" at the end of their TV show could dispel the apocalyptic vibe that was in the air. In 1954 Roman Catholics observed the Marian Year, and with it, rumors that the Virgin's final message at Fatima was about to be revealed to Pope Pius XII. In some tellings the pope already knew the message, but was withholding it to avoid causing worldwide panic. We Protestants felt our own latter-days darkness lurking at the margins of American prosperity: a sense that souls had to be won to Jesus before the bomb came and it was too late to convert anyone—including yourself, if you were a doubter. Wasn't God smiting the Russians with alcoholism and unemployment to punish them for rejecting Jesus? The fifties saw the rise of radio and TV preachers who espoused this very blend of patriotism and piety: the apex of the American Century was also the ascendant age of Billy Graham.

Protestant versus Catholic tensions in our small town took the form of mutual bewilderment and the occasional tasteless joke. We Protestant kids were convinced that Catholics worshiped statues and prayed to the pope rather than to Jesus. I can only imagine what the Catholic kids thought about us, with our hysterical preachers and our fitful attempts to parse the Bible for ourselves, like jaybirds trying to read the *Toledo Blade*. All sectarian differences disappeared, however, in our mutual opposition to those godless Communists. Didn't Khrushchev promise to "bury" all of us? And hadn't the Russians shut down the churches and forced people to worship Lenin's stuffed body? During the fifties many Americans believed that the antonym of Communism was not capitalism, but Christianity. In 1954 Congress concurred by inserting the phrase "under God" into the Pledge of Allegiance.

Although my parents refused to push this hysteria onto their kids, I knew from my grandmother, a militant Methodist and a biblical literalist, that if I didn't get right with Jesus before the bomb came, I'd be in eternal hot water. And because I never *did* get right with Jesus, at least not to my satisfaction, religion remained a mostly scary thing: at best a constant reprimand, at worst an unspoken terror. Knowing which way Toledo lay, I sometimes avoided looking north. I didn't want to see the mushroom cloud when it rose, because then I'd know that in a few seconds Jesus and a fireball would be blowing through, hand in hand. It would be better not to see either of them coming.

Religion has always functioned as a collective antidote to the existential terror of being human—to what Cambridge anthropologist Jane Harrison once called "fear felt together." Sometimes, however, religion backfires by whipping up the very fear that it is supposed to assuage. This usually happens when the spiritual impulse stops moving like the biblical wind and hardens into a collection of believe-it-or-die certitudes. I can attest from childhood experience that this kind of hardening creates fear felt alone, which is not a pleasant emotion. I've often considered it fortunate that I never owned any of the religious playsets that were around at the time. What fun is a toy that you're afraid to look at, let alone play with?

Given the grip of religion on the postwar imagination, America's toymakers could not afford to ignore it. The Marx company produced a boxed set of Jesus and the apostles, a Nativity set, a Noah's Ark playset (a rival set came from the Auburn Rubber company), a Ben Hur playset, and a Ten Commandments playset complete with three different Moseses. Marx also issued a number of figures in the same commemorative 60-millimeter format as their presidents—and here, too, piety and patriotism went hand in hand. In addition to the western heroes and American generals, these figures included yet another Moses, Pope Pius XII, and Cardinal Spellman of New York. Other religious figures produced by Marx included the two Friar Tucks at 54-millimeter and 60-millimeter scale, a Bible-toting chaplain that came with the early "medical" G.I.s, and a missionary that was included in the Jungle Jim playset but dropped from the later Daktari set, perhaps for skimming the collection plate.

The Jungle Jim missionary embodied the prevailing fifties assumption that genuine religiosity was Christian and white. This dignified figure in khaki shorts, cast in cream soft plastic and holding an open Bible, contrasted tellingly with the half-naked witch doctor, cast in brown, who writhed orgiastically in a lion-head mask. Still, the Marx designers may have maintained at least some distance from the ideology that they were promoting, because the jungle accessories included a suspiciously large, missionary-ready cooking pot. Did the inclusion of this pot reflect Marx's secret solidarity with the kind of dissent that Senator McCarthy and the House Un-American Activities Committee were trying to stamp out? Or, as is more likely, was the pot a simple concession to the old saw that boys will be boys? As the kind of boy who hated going to church, I would have been tempted to cook the missionary when Grandma wasn't looking. I wouldn't have been the only one to consider doing so, either: artist David Levinthal, in his 1996 collection of photographs of Marx figures, posed the Jungle Jim missionary in just this manner.

The Marx company left no such opening for irreverent play with Jesus and the apostles. Indeed, this collection of 60-millimeter saints was not marketed as an ordinary playset; instead, the box identified them as "religious figurines." Jesus and the apostles are fairly hard to find today, especially in mint condition. Molded in the same brittle plastic as the commemorative figures and the presidents, some of the apostles had delicate, finger-pointing hands and thin staffs that were easily broken. When you do find Jesus and the apostles, however, the original box is frequently still with them—far more often than is the case with other playsets. The reason seems obvious: children must have played with these figures carefully and even reverently, re-boxing them like prized chessmen after each session. I can't imagine any dirt-clod wars between Peter's team and John's team, or elaborately staged crashes in which Christian saints tumble down the stairs in a canvas-topped army truck. No American boy in the fifties, not even a church-hating one, would dare subject Jesus and the apostles to such indignities.

As a child I would have found the very notion of a Jesus and the Apostles playset disturbing. Wouldn't a playtime reminder of Grandma's hellfire stifle any fun? A bit braver now, I'm studying the full set that stands before me. The box boldly asserts that these figures are "lifelike"; if this claim is true, the Marx designers were more visionary than even the most enthusiastic toy collectors insist. The set contains fifteen figures: Jesus, of course; thirteen disciples, including Judas and his replacement Matthias; and Paul, not one of the twelve but so prominent a figure in early Christianity that he could scarcely be omitted. Each apostle has his name on the front of his base, a brief description on the back, and a heraldic shield underneath. The lettering of these inscriptions is tiny: although the back of Matthew's base reads "Also Called Levi," a nearsighted eBay seller once described this figure as "also called Lew." Judas is the only figure whose base contains nothing on the reverse or bottom, arguably the most chilling example of significant absence in the history of toy design.

While these figures might not be verifiably "lifelike" as apostolic portraits, they are certainly true to life in another respect: their thick substantiality reflects the 1950s American link between piety and prosperity. Although Marx could have issued waiflike embodiments of otherworldliness and saved materials costs in the bargain, these figures are well-fed exemplars of worldly as well as spiritual success. Their faces, though reasonably individualized, share a basic type: the broad, burly faces of working men also found on the 60-millimeter Robin Hood figures.

Except for John, who is young and beardless, the Marx apostles are all middle-aged and beyond. These are not the scruffy sectarians who followed the historical Jesus, but the revered sages of later Christianity—and they are faithful, for the most part, to their iconographic traditions. The only exception is Paul: unlike the balding figure in most ancient and medieval depictions, the Marx Paul has a full head of wavy hair, like Gordon MacRae. Jesus, of course, looks exactly like Jesus—or more precisely, the Anglo-Nordic Jesus of the American popular imagination in the fifties. This is the Jesus whose portrait hung on the walls of my Sunday school classrooms and graced the cover of the *Upper Room*, a monthly magazine of daily Bible meditations to which Grandma subscribed. This is definitely not the risen Jesus, whose picture in my childhood copy of *Hurlbut's Story of the Bible* terrified me because he gleamed like a ghost. Nor is it the apocalyptic Jesus returning for revenge—the Jesus whom I was afraid to see standing some night at the foot of my bed, backlit by a nuclear glow issuing from Toledo.

Seen in theological terms, the Marx Jesus is not the judge, but the advocate: the Jesus who forgives everyone and is good with children. This figure might indeed have eased my childhood fears because it represents the insider's Jesus, the one whom believers claim to know and expect someday to see. I suspect that playing with this figure in a respectful manner made a child feel like this sort of insider. Wouldn't playtime confidence in being numbered among the sheep rather than the goats make for a happy consumer? And yet, this business of finding exactly what we're seeking has deeper implications. Whenever the Virgin appears, whether in a grotto or on the side of a building, she is perfectly recognizable. If she failed to accord with our preconceived image of her, there would be no report of an apparition, just some shepherd kids heading back home or a workman painting over a vaguely humanlike shape on a wall. When it came to fulfilling collective expectations, the Marx designers did not disappoint: by reproducing the image of Jesus that prevailed in the American fifties, they put a powerful cultural idea into concrete, legible form.

We postwar sinners may have needed this kind of clarity, with all the getting and spending that was going on—all those Elvis records, Frigidaires, and Thunderbirds that we were heaping onto our heads. Materialism, we knew, was a sinful philosophy: even Saint Lew could attest to that. A redemptive upside to all this mass consumption, however, lay in the ancient theological dictum that grace would be meaningless—even inconceivable—without sin. In this view, Adam and Eve committed a felix culpa, a fall that was "happy" because it made divine forgiveness possible. The New Testament seemed to reinforce the spiritual utility of sin when Jesus told Judas to "do what you have to do" in order to let the divine sacrifice go forward. Postwar materialism found similar justification in a surfeited reaction against itself, in its own negative echo of mirroring culpability. To be sure, the fifties dad was not thinking about God when he plugged in that expensive new hi-fi. Almost immediately, however, the bliss of hearing Sinatra with fresh ears triggered sufficient guilt to make him repent of buying it, if only for a moment.

Maybe I'm wrong in counting myself lucky to have missed the Marx Jesus and the apostles as a child. By making my transgressions seem as necessary to the cosmic order as the phases of the moon or our family's new Ford Fairlane, these figures might have eased my guilt as a stubborn holdout who could never be sure whether or not he believed. I'm looking at the Marx Judas now, and the accursed figure with the blank underside is doing exactly the bad-kid thing that we would expect: he's clutching a bag of coins. Had I owned Judas as a child, I might have taken comfort from projecting my fear of a nuclear Jesus onto him. "Yes I'm bad," I could have said, "but I'm not as bad as *this* guy." I could have sent Judas down the stairs in an army truck and gone to bed self-righteous and ready for the bomb, conveniently ignoring the fact that my parents had dipped into their own bag of coins to buy him for me.

As Judas's presence suggests, these "religious figurines" operated like any other playset, in that bad guys were necessary sources of conflict, and therefore of story. Within the toy realm, however, the clearest manifestation of sin is not evil thoughts or deeds, but mistakes in molding or design—and here it was not Judas who erred, but Jesus himself. Marx initially released the set with Jesus raising his left hand in blessing. Like 15 percent of the population, I'm left-handed; had the mistake gone unnoticed, we southpaws would finally have had a Jesus of our own, a savior for sinners living in a perpetual mirror. But Louis Marx didn't become the Toy King by catering to aggrieved minorities. Knowing that cultural icons were not to be tampered with, that you had to get them right, Louis Marx staged a Second Playset Coming: a reissued set with a corrected Jesus who gave the proper, right-handed blessing. As if to atone for their mistake, the Marx designers made Second Coming Jesus almost a quarter of an inch taller than his predecessor. The revised Jesus also looks older and more careworn than the first version—it's as if he has absorbed the trouble and expense of his own retooling.

I'm still wondering how children actually played with Jesus and the apostles. Given their static poses, these figures could be put on display, like our mothers' Hummel doll collections or those large-scale, obsessively detailed horses that our sisters loved. But little boys must have felt an impulse to take things further. The most immediate option, perhaps, would be to make toy apostles spread the Word to other playset figures. It's easy to imagine a warm reception among the battle-weary Marx soldiers; the response of the 60-millimeter Romans and the 54-millimeter Ben Hur figures might be cooler. The Marx dinosaurs would probably remain utterly indifferent, scarcely looking up from their grazing and thus unwittingly sealing their extinction. A child with exceptional biblical literacy could also make the apostles tip each other over, thereby reenacting their debate in the Gospels over who is the greatest among them; Jesus could then restore calm before everyone returned to the box. Or perhaps Peter and Paul could be transported to the Ben Hur amphitheater to reenact their traditional martyrdoms, though both are too stately to replicate an inverted crucifixion or a beheading. The Marx apostles can stand up or lie down, but that's it: they can be alive or dead, but nothing in between.

And therein lies a paradox. By depicting stories that were already deemed fixed and inalterable, religious playsets discouraged any real play. Wouldn't the invention of genuinely new stories for such toys lead to playtime irreverence? The Marx designers seem to have recognized this danger: by walking on eggshells with their ultra-conventional Jesus and the apostles, they chose stasis over action and boredom over blasphemy. Two decades later, the Atlantic toy company of Italy would make a different choice by issuing a playset that refused to leave unanswered the question of how a child might play with little Christians. Atlantic infused action into their Christians and Gladiators set by supplying little martyrs-to-be, including a mother holding an infant in her arms; clearly, children were supposed to rescue these hapless figures from the fiercely gesticulating gladiators. Still, the set could not overcome the limitations of religious toys. These little Christians, permanent sufferers like those writhing Saint Sebastians in baroque churches, posed a maddeningly simple choice: the child could either save them or kill them, thumbs up or thumbs down. Like the Marx Jesus and the Apostles set, the Atlantic Christians and Gladiators set failed as a toy because it had only one story to tell.

Other toymakers have tried to solve this problem. At first glance, a David and Goliath playset issued in 1996 by Rainfall Educational Toys seems promising. The set contains forty-eight Israelite and Philistine warriors, a 2-inch David, a 4-inch Goliath, and a "parent/teacher guide" that explains the developmental benefits of playsets for five- to ten-year-olds, provides information on ancient weaponry, and contains an expanded paraphrase of the biblical story in 1 Samuel along with some theological lessons to be drawn from it. Although this set promises traditional playset action in a fight to the death, it suffers from the same restrictions as Atlantic's Christians and Gladiators. David leans backwards with loaded sling while Goliath stares fiercely and waits; a child can make David's stone hit the giant or miss him, but only one outcome is really possible. Who would dare let the Philistines win?

Other recent attempts to infuse religious toys with genuine play value include an 11-inch Jesus made by a company called One2Believe; this figure speaks one of six passages from the Gospels of Mark and John when its back is pressed. In a recent eBay auction that paired this talking Jesus with a talking Moses who recites the Ten Commandments, the seller coaxed viewers to bid on "Law & Grace in one package." But here, too, the limits on play are strict, reduced to a simple choice of either heeding these figures or not—and in a pious home, the latter option would be unthinkable. Other toy Jesuses of recent manufacture appear somewhat less restrictive. Two 5-inch figures stand on wheels: one has posable arms, while the other has glow-in-the-dark hands and comes with a wine jug and some loaves and fishes. Although the wheels certainly correct the stasis of the old Marx Jesus, the resulting "action" might be too physical for these figures to be "religious" in any recognizable sense. Rolling a toy Jesus across a kitchen floor might be fun, but it's difficult to imagine how doing so would deepen a child's faith. And that's the inescapable trade-off. With too little action, the religious toy loses its essence as a toy and becomes a static confirmation of piety. With too much action, or with action conceived too literally, the religious toy risks becoming just another toy. At least a Jesus on wheels can move—and shouldn't spiritual play involve movement of some sort, a shattering of rigid pieties by opening things up a little? The Marx company missed an opportunity to generate such play when they gave Jesus and the apostles such inert, hieratic poses. By playset standards, these figures were duds: they just stood there, as they're standing here now. But to be fair, what choice did the company have? Especially in the fifties, Jesus and the apostles had a predetermined, static iconography that could not be tampered with. The Marx Nativity set, though a commercial success, had the same problem: as with any other crèche, once you set up Marx's version there was little else to do but look at it. A Last Supper playset, had the company issued one, would have been similarly constrained. Once you replicated the Leonardo da Vinci fresco by arranging the figures at a hard-plastic table, complete with an overturned saltshaker in front of Judas, all play would pretty much cease. I suppose that you could make the bad-boy disciple slink out of the scene to do what he had to do, but what then?

As for those "lifelike" apostles, the very notion of realism makes sense only in relation to a perceptible reality. Secular playset figures appeal to this reality with varying degrees of success: we can judge how "realistic" toy cowboys and soldiers are by comparing them to actual cowboys and soldiers. Toy figures of religious people also pose no problem, so long as they are actual people. We know, for instance, what Pope Pius XII looked like; his playset version, which I acquired for twenty-five dollars, closely resembles the old photographs. But what should a playset apostle look like? A 60-millimeter figure with Gordon MacRae hair might conceivably offer an accurate depiction of a first-century Jewish tentmaker from Tarsus, though we have no way of knowing for sure. But tradition holds that Saul the tentmaker was transformed on the road to Damascus into the Paul the apostle—and while the Marx Paul exists to commemorate the latter role, it is precisely this role that a playset figure cannot portray. Because Paul the apostle has been imagined and reimagined over centuries of Christian reflection, a playset Paul can only be a representation of prior representations. As such, the figure will not embody transcendence, but history: its stubborn materiality will always pull it back into the contingent realms of time and space. This is why the Marx apostles, however piously posed, look less like agents of spiritual transformation than a bunch of middle-aged men in robes.

Of course, anyone who has spent years teaching and writing about religious literature, as I have, might be too hard to please. Not only is it silly to take toys—even religious ones—too seriously, but the apostles' reduction to hard plastic probably granted a measure of agency to the children who tried, even with mixed success, to play with them. The more I think about it, the more I envy those kids. Having a set of plastic apostles under my control might have eased some childhood terrors. Jesus might have seemed less scary if I had gotten to know him at a manageable, 60-millimeter scale.

Better late than never. As I study the Marx Jesus and the apostles now, their impact is like recalling a bad dream but remembering, all over again, that it was only a dream. Typical fifties artifacts in their blend of piety and commerce, these figures seem to have become better toys for having been desanctified by the passage of time. Their central figure does not depict Christ—how could it?—but it could conceivably depict the earthly Jesus, at least as he was imagined when I was little. And while I still don't have a handle on the transcendent Christ, the earthly Jesus is a different matter altogether, a subject of intense and longstanding interest. What's more, Marx's decision to match a young-man Jesus with middle-aged apostles has made these toys ideal for some grown-up play. With their portly physiques and inert poses, it is easy to identify with them, especially my plastic look-alike, Simon the Zealot. A hot-headed action figure when young, Simon now stands on my desk with a dazed expression and a staff broken at both ends.

While I can't be sure whether Simon and his companions would have terrified or comforted me as a child, I can certainly play with them now. Indeed, I can't *not* play with them. My connection to Simon and the rest of this desktop crowd is allowing these old toys to make all sorts of incursions into my non-collecting life. One of the things that I do in that life is teach a course in the Gospels—no great surprise, perhaps, given my obsession with Left-Handed Jesus. It's not easy to separate the English professor from the toy collector, and sometimes I don't even try. The last time I taught the course, I fell into a new ritual: as I prepared for each class, I lined up Jesus and the apostles on my desk and pretended that they were exhorting me to generate deeper and more engaging discussions of their story. Maybe these figures have achieved their intended goal after all. Aren't they proving themselves capable of stimulating some kind of inner "action," even though they're standing perfectly still?

At this moment, for instance, they are prompting a fantasy in which I've just been ushered into a plush office at the Marx corporate headquarters on Fifth Avenue. I'm here to pitch a new product to the boss himself: a Transfiguration playset. As Louis Marx calmly puffs on a cigar, I enthusiastically explain that this set would include a plastic mountain, similar to the vacuum-formed rocks that came with the Prehistoric Times playset, with niches on the top for three figures: Moses, Elijah, and a fiercely inapproachable, glow-in-the-dark Jesus.

Peter, James, and John would all be cast in rubbery vinyl so they could swoon and tumble down the mountain, over and over, and not break under their perpetual rediscovery of human limitations.

When Marx asks about the set's play value, I have a ready answer: these repeated reenactments of the disciples' endless rise and fall—a biblical version of old Sisyphus and his immense rock—would surely become a child's most cherished private ritual. It would *have* to be private, too, because according to the Gospel story, the three witnesses to the event were sworn to secrecy. Kids couldn't use this set as a lure to get friends to come over and play: this is one toy that would have to be played with alone and in utter silence. And because such play might get a little scary, the glow-in-the-dark Jesus would be joined by an additional Jesus, the southpaw who blesses each of my new arrivals. Benignly goofy in his mirrorlike confusion, Left-Handed Jesus would stand close at hand for much the same reason that he stands here on my desk: as a reminder that despite all the wars and rumors of wars, the smaller pleasures of life are not likely to go up in a mushroom cloud anytime soon.

Wincing slightly at my mention of Left-Handed Jesus, the Toy King politely listens until I finish my pitch. Then he hesitates a moment before delivering the hard truth: a Transfiguration playset would be a complete flop, a commercial disaster. Marx gently explains that you can't make money from a toy that would appeal to a single consumer—especially a broody one. After all, play is supposed to be fun. Aware of my disappointment, the boss leads me into a showroom filled with his current products, points toward a shelf filled with religious toys, and invites me to choose one of them to take home, free of charge.

It's a shame that this is only a fantasy: whatever I chose would have been the equivalent of a ground-floor share in Microsoft. In their unflappable serenity, the Marx Jesus and the apostles confirm the biblical promise that whoever remains faithful unto the end will be rewarded a hundredfold. A full set, mint with box, usually sells on eBay for between $100 and $150—although my set, I hasten to add, cost only $50 because of Simon's broken staff and some torn flaps on the box. A Left-Handed Jesus, at $20 to $25, is more valuable than a Second Coming Jesus, though not excessively so; a lot of flawed sets must have left the plant before the mistake was spotted.

While the Gospel is pricy, the Law is pricier: the 60-millimeter commemorative Moses, on those rare occasions when it appears on eBay, sells for around $1000. The Ten Commandments set, with its smaller Moseses in three poses, usually fetches $300 to $500. The current value of the Ten Commandments set is at odds with the economics of playset interchangeability that went into its production: several of the apostles, having renounced their Christian beliefs and undergone a downscaling to one and a half inches, were recycled here as wandering Hebrews. Even Judas, his money bag painted over to make it less prominent, is making the trek out of Egypt. I do not own the Ten Commandments playset or the 60-millimeter commemoratives of Moses and Cardinal Spellman. Covetous but not insane when such figures are offered for sale, I watch in fear and trembling as the bids grow and the winner emerges, doubtless another middle-aged man seeking some sort of redemption. Anyone who pays $80 for a two-and-a-half-inch Pope Pius XII, as one eBay buyer recently did, must be trying to live down an unsaved fifties boyhood even more desperately than I am.

Getting and Spending . . . .

Quizzical Al deserves his prominent place toward the front of the desktop crowd. The first playset figures of my childhood, Marx dinosaurs also prompted my adult obsession with old toys when I got on eBay, entered a search for "vintage dinosaurs," and encountered pictures of my half-forgotten Jurassic pets. For a while, simply knowing that they were still in the world brought ample reassurance, but then the whole point of eBay hit me: I could actually *have* them again.

Like all addicts, I started small, bidding only on the first series dinosaurs that I once owned. But as soon as I discovered how appealing the second series figures were, I wanted them, too. Then I wanted to have every figure in green and gray, their most common colors. Once I learned that the dinosaurs also came in flat brown, a fact unknown to me as a child, I had to have every figure in three colors. Eventually I came across an even rarer color, flat tan, with predictable results. Other animals soon followed: the Auburn Rubber farm and jungle sets led to the Marx Prized Livestock, which led to more animals by Marx and by the Multiple Products Corporation. Then came the human figures—and here, too, I worked from memory outward: from toy people that I owned as a child to figures that I had never seen before. Ravishing Dale led to Standing Roy, who led to Pat Brady and the Mineral City cowboys, who led to the 60-millimeter Marx Combat G.I.s, who led to the 45-millimeter soldiers and sailors from the Armed Forces Training Center, who led to 54-millimeter Battlefield soldiers, who led to the Marx presidents. With the acquisition of several Auburn Rubber soldiers, I had reached the end of the line in reclaiming my childhood toys. These figures look just as I remember them: didn't I once know their faces by heart? Every time I pick one up, however, I am surprised—all over again—by how small and light it is, how differently it fits in my hand.

It was the Marx presidents who coaxed me into the company of strangers, starting with the similarly sculpted Marx generals. The generals in turn led to the 60-millimeter Civil War figures, who led to the 54-millimeter Civil War figures, who led to the Robin Hood knights in both scales, and on, and on. Along the way I discovered that Marx was not the only manufacturer of interesting figures. Auburn Rubber produced a splendid series of pioneers, Indians, and civilian workers: how could I not have them, too—along with those nicely detailed sailors, soldiers, and knights made by Ideal? And how could I restrict myself to collecting American toys once I learned that appealing figures were also made in England (by Britains and Cherilea), Italy (by Atlantic), and Spain (by Jecsan and Reamsa)? As more pieces of vintage vinyl and plastic came into the house, the population of my desktop world grew like Las Vegas in the nineties. As in Las Vegas, newcomers far outnumber indigenous inhabitants: as a child I owned only sixteen of the 150-odd figures standing before me. Among the figures stored in plastic bags, the ratio of owned to un-owned pieces is roughly the same as on this desktop: about one in ten.

My collecting story has been a narrative of expanding desire, like the building of Rome but faster—and it was familiar to the old hands whom I met during my dinosaur hunt, when I was just starting out. Despite the popular image, collectors of vintage toys are not feral losers incapable of human interaction. On the contrary, the realm of Marx dinosaur hunters proved to be surprisingly sociable: a band of brothers—yes, we were overwhelmingly male—united in our love for these old figures but fully aware of the obsessive nature of this love. Most of the dinosaur collectors with whom I corresponded were in their fifties, and all possessed postwar American-boy nicknames: Dave from Detroit, Mike from Indiana, Rich from Wheeling, Bill from Missouri, Rick from Pennsylvania, and another Rick from Cleveland.

As we bought and sold and traded, other stories emerged—though gradually and tentatively, in keeping with midlife-male reticence. Dave told how he once buried his dinosaurs in his mother's garden for a future archaeological dig, but then forgot the exact spot. When his mother replaced them with a set of MPC dinosaurs—*not the same!*—he remained heartbroken until he rediscovered his Marx dinosaurs by chance. Mike confessed to an incremental addiction similar to mine, though his collecting went even further: a few loose figures, then a complete playset or two, then as many playsets as he could find, and finally a part-time business buying and selling old toys nationwide. For Pennsylvania Rick, the news editor at a small-town paper, a boyhood love of Marx dinosaurs led to a second career as an amateur paleontologist. A collector of toy dinosaurs as well as an expert on the real things, he is currently overseeing the excavation of the largest Late Triassic site ever discovered in the mid-Atlantic region.

When I started to collect playset people, I met other midlife seekers, many of whom had developed minute specialties: in militaria, historical figures, toy company history, European figures, the Civil War, and so on. There is considerable learning here. Allan from Pennsylvania, an expert on playset representations of history, comments knowledgeably on anachronisms in the weaponry and armor of ancient and medieval figures. Kent from Florida is an expert on production histories: which figures were included in what mold, how the molds were retooled for different sets, and where the molds went after the manufacturers went bankrupt. Jim from Massachusetts possesses a scholar's knowledge of military figures produced in the forties and fifties; his eBay listings offer an advanced education in toy soldier evolution.

For some collectors, a playset figure is not simply an object to admire, but a medium of self-expression, an artist's canvas to be painted with meticulous care and historical accuracy. These figures are advertised with claims like "Marx Romans, custom painted with authentic colors of the Legio III Gallica!" Other collectors create "conversions," heating and bending limbs and necks to form variant poses—in effect, creating new collecting opportunities for those who already own complete sets. The most interesting conversion that I've acquired is an Atlantic Trojan whose head has been carefully grafted from an Atlantic Greek. This figure embodies an alternative history: what if Troy had been the site not of a ten-year siege, but of ten summers of love? It also poses a dilemma to the collector's rage for order: should a Greek-headed Trojan be stored in the Greek bag or the Trojan bag?

Toy collectors often make comically self-deprecating remarks that seem to stem from vague sheepishness at the whole enterprise. Two themes pervade our conversations. The first is the wistful nostalgia common to middle-aged men who are getting their old toys back: our sentences often begin with "My friends and I used to. . . ." Missouri Bill once made the sadness inherent in collecting old toys explicit when he altered a quote—and the meter—from "Men with Broken Hearts," a 1950 song by Hank Williams in his "Luke the Drifter" persona: "Souls that live within the past, where sorrow plays all parts, / Where a living death is all that's left for toy collectors with broken hearts." The second common theme of our talk is bad-boy glee, expressed in occasional comments about how "the wife" doesn't understand how cool this stuff is, but "puts up with it" anyway. Although this wife-as-mom motif is a little creepy, the melancholy and mischief are inseparable. Even as we grieve for the boys whom we left behind by growing up, these old toys reanimate the enthusiasm that those boys once felt toward weird little objects whose appeal was—and remains—incomprehensible to outsiders.

How does this enthusiasm feel? As my collection of playset figures grows, the satisfactions of arranging them just so—then just so another way—are sufficiently powerful to be embarrassing. I often feel as if I'm breaking into the odd sense of timelessness and placelessness that I recall from childhood. At my bidding, the 60-millimeter Little John tells a joke that makes a Mineral City outlaw forget why his gun is drawn. An Ideal knight debates energy policy with a Marx Arab from the Captain Gallant set, then rides off on an MPC elephant. Sitting Roy rides absurdly atop what for him is the dog-sized (but in Greek, "dog-jawed") cynognathus, while Bullet jealously looks on. Calvin Coolidge, hat in hand, flirts with a Marx dollhouse mother and Mrs. Noah from the Auburn Rubber ark set, while the megatheria that the trio rode in on converse in a nearby paddock. These old figures are generating new stories, just as they were originally meant to do—and the possibilities seem infinite. Yes, I think to myself, this is worth it.

That is, until it isn't. One evening I found myself idly tracking an eBay auction for ten 54-millimeter Alamo/Fort Apache pioneers. These are by no means rare figures: I had won a full set several months earlier for eleven dollars. As the auction neared its end, however, this routine event exploded into a display of acquisitive fervor such as one rarely confronts in everyday life. After a last-minute flurry of bids, the winning price was $410.

Why would anyone pay over $400 for ten Marx pioneers, when nearly complete Alamo or Fort Apache playsets can be had for between $150 and $200? Did these figures possess some obscure cachet that I was too unschooled to appreciate? I retrieved my pioneers from their plastic bag and searched, in vain, for some arcane feature that might account for that price: specks of gold leaf on coat buttons, perhaps, or tiny Nostradamus prophecies stamped on the bases. Nor could I discover an in-joke known only to playset experts: Louis Marx's features, for example, did not appear on any of these faces. Granted, my pioneers were not color matched and several gun barrels were shortened, but such flaws cannot explain a $399 price difference. Something deeply personal must have been going on: maybe the pioneer carrying the wild turkey reminded a bidder of a Thanksgiving memory involving his long-dead father. But then I remembered that it takes at least two people to generate bidding insanity. How likely was it that the turkey-carrying pioneer reminded two people of two dead fathers on two distant Thanksgivings?

The bidders' real motives were probably related less to their personal histories than to the adrenaline rush of competition: simply put, neither one could bear the thought of losing. Although the clichéd aftermath of their competition—a loser's agony and a winner's ecstasy—seems obvious, I am imagining a more complicated outcome. At the decisive moment, both bidders are ecstatic: just as the winner shouts "They're mine!" to an empty room, the loser rejoices at making that sucker pay through the nose. And yet, I'd be willing to bet that by the time they turned off their computers, both bidders felt unaccountably sad. The loser would of course lament not getting his prize, but the winner's distress would be greater, especially after checking several completed auctions and discovering the usual price for 54-millimeter pioneers.

I had in that event witnessed raw hysteria, an online reincarnation of the Dutch tulip craze of the seventeenth century or the Florida real estate boom of the twenties. The more I thought about it, the more my sense of superiority to these fools got replaced by those classic responses to tragedy: fear and pity. The pity came first: I had just watched twin Oedipuses putting out their own eyes. The fear arose more gradually, and assumed its scariest form as a question: I've never been Oedipus, have I?

The line between toys that would be nice to get and toys that you *must* get keeps shifting, because "nice" turns into need before you know it. Is $20 too much to pay for a 60-millimeter Pat Brady? On one particular day I thought not, though now I'm not so sure. Like the middle-aged guys—they *had* to be middle-aged guys—who fought over those pioneers, I have a history, too. With equal parts of elation and shame, I once paid $91 for fifteen dinosaurs that included three rarities: a tyrannosaurus, brontosaurus, and kronosaurus in the older, flat brown. Although these figures were in perfect shape and I was overjoyed to get them, they also suggest a disturbing answer to that question about Oedipus.

Seen dispassionately, bidding for old toys on eBay is a thinly disguised arcade game, a first cousin to cyber-gambling: the need to win can take you where wise men fear to tread. But collecting is hardly a dispassionate enterprise. Collectors are not motivated chiefly by a desire to possess things, but by a deeper obsession with completeness, with self-contained wholes. It's not enough to own every Mineral City cowboy except the outlaw with his hands up: you must acquire that outlaw even if he costs more than all the others combined. This fetish for completeness is not just quantitative. Once you get the outlaw, you'll grow increasingly impatient with the split rope of your lassoing rider and start seeking a better exemplar of *him*. And once you score a mint lassoing rider, you'll gaze in satisfaction at your complete, mint set of Mineral City cowboys until it occurs to you, after about five minutes, that it would be nice to have a backup set.

I draw some consolation from knowing that the winner of those pioneers is worse off than I am. When I checked his eBay buying record, I learned that he routinely spends insane amounts, usually for toys with their original boxes or header cards. Most of these items were never opened: he likes his old toys brand new, devoid of prior human contact. In the weeks leading up to the Battle for the Pioneers, he spent $40 for one unassembled Fort Apache block house with its original bag, $48.77 for Marx's second-series farm animals in their original box, $160.49 for a missile set still on its header card, and $202.50 for an unassembled Marx Happi-Time Farm, factory-flat in the box.

Original packaging—especially if unopened—is a widespread obsession. I have watched several YouTube videos of middle-aged men opening vintage, factory-stapled Marx playsets for the camera. These clips have the feel of delivery-room footage: the careful unwrapping of each playset component prompts expressions of wonder and relief. "Clean, clean, clean," exclaimed an affable expert after his friend gently pried open a Marx Untouchables box and exposed the lithographed tin packed beneath the top flap. At first, the friend was alarmed that the gangsters were in blue and the cops were in gray, but the expert reminded him of the value of an inverted-color set: "Rare, rare, rare!" Granted, these guys were making a lot out of a little—but I identified with them completely, and was pleased that they were happy with their find. Disappointment, of course, is always possible. In another video, a collector discovered that the tin-litho in his freshly opened Marx Modern Doll House had been corroded by moisture. He received another unpleasant surprise when he opened the bag that contained the patio furniture: "Uh-oh. There's no barbeque grill."

I respect these people for their knowledge: they know exactly what they have, or don't. The pioneers winner is a different sort of collector altogether—the kind who freely spends but knows not what he gets. I noticed that this man consistently overpays even for loose pieces that are not rarities: $23.80 for two Auburn steers and a calf, for instance, a grouping that usually sells for $10 to $15. Another time he paid $46.05 for nine 54-millimeter cowboys, three horses, and a steer; the combined price for these items usually runs between $15 and $25. And although Nellybelle, Pat Brady's Jeep, is a relatively scarce item that usually fetches $40 to $50, the pioneers winner paid $92.50 for his. He is also impatient with the uncertain outcomes of competitive bidding: he once did a Buy It Now at $399.99 for a Marx Mike Hazard Double Agent doll, an item that usually goes for between $50 and $100.

Could this man's money have been better spent? Anyone who has paid almost a hundred dollars to acquire three flat-brown dinosaurs cannot answer this question objectively. I will say, however, that the pioneers winner is missing out on the two main benefits of collecting old toys. The first is that the hobby can teach you things: about the toys and their era, of course, but also about yourself—and wildly indiscriminate spending hardly reflects genuine introspection. The second is that old toys connect you with other people from other times. This is why I'd rather own a figure with playwear than a mint one:

knowing that children once consecrated these objects with their love is, for me, a sappy but irresistible part of their charm. What's more, the mint-in-the-box crowd, who wouldn't dream of opening original packaging and instantly reducing an item's value by half, create a depressing trap for themselves. Once you've acquired a coveted, unopened thing, what can you *do* with it? The answer, of course, is nothing, except to store it in a cool, dry place—a 60-millimeter tomb— until you either sell it or enter your own tomb and your heirs sell it. There's something chilling about collecting unplayed-with toys: it's like rehearsing your own death.

It's tempting to dismiss the pioneers winner as a crazy person. In the desire-driven world of eBay, however, it is the crazy people who determine the final prices. On the day following the pioneers auction, somebody put up a nearly identical set with a starting bid of $175. And why not? At least one angry loser was still out there, desperate to redeem his disappointment.

Any good Buddhist can tell you that desire makes us vulnerable— and when we're vulnerable, it can be a Daktari Jungle out there. Or as the Ben Hur Romans might put it, *caveat emptor.* Shrewd sellers understand a collector's weaknesses. Some play dumb but cover their bases, posting figures cast in garish colors and waxy plastic with come-ons like "Might be recasts, but look like originals to me." Also common is the folksy ploy, which often involves a poignant family narrative. Whenever you read "Must sell Grandpa's old toys: I hope these bring joy into another child's life" and there is an opening bid of $39.99 with a high reserve price, you can bet not only that "Grandpa" himself is sitting at the computer, but that he regularly consults Richard O'Brien's *Collecting Toys,* Tim Geppert's *Guide to Non-Metallic Toy Soldiers of the U.S.,* and back issues of *Plastic Figure and Playset Collector* magazine. Cheap figures made in China since the eighties generate the most frequent protestations of seller ignorance. The standard disclaimer—"I don't know anything about these"—is often followed by the magic phrase: "Might be Marx."

The reliable sellers, usually professional dealers in antique toys, go to the opposite extreme, providing their hobbyist clientele with item descriptions that are scrupulous to a fault: "Indians a deeper red than photo shows," or "Third G.I. from left has unmarked base." Such recitations of exactitude read like found poems: "Scuffed nose on axe-man"; "Farmer's wife has difficulty standing"; "Near-perfect color match, but two chewed swords." These sellers often speak with an insider's code, the clipped argot of the aficionado: "Training Center Camp Poses, OD rubber, C-8"; "45mm Dearborns with Mint Scalper"; "Matched Chubbies, No Splits." These knowledgeable sellers are also buyers, of course, and before eBay started hiding bidders' identities, you could learn who these cooler heads were and follow their lead. Not only were their bids reasonable guides to, well, what's reasonable, but an absence of their bids contained its own eloquence.

There's a taxonomy of buyers, too: by our bids ye shall know us. The casual bidder, who relies on sheer luck and other people's negligence, enters low bids on many lots but seems content never to win one. His antithesis is the slam-dunk "sniper," to use eBay parlance, who doesn't bid until punching in an exorbitant amount at the last minute; this type wins a lot, but pays a lot. I would call myself an ordinary, mid-range eBay type: the classic two-stage bidder. I usually test the waters early with an initial bid, and then make a second, earnest bid near—but not at—the auction's close. Although I used to snipe fairly regularly, I soon learned that sniping contains an unavoidable danger: the existence of another sniper. As ten 54-millimeter pioneers somewhere in the world can attest, two people shooting for the moon in the final seconds can rocket a price to insane levels.

Some prospective buyers, eager to display their expertise, ask sellers arcane questions or make know-it-all corrections to listings: "These colors look a little bright: I'd say these are Heritage figures," or "The bazooka man is actually by Ideal." The replies of sellers, who are also proud of what they know, sometimes result in playset-lore testosterone fests: "Been collecting 20 years: definitely NOT Heritage." The most experienced sellers, however, refuse to take the bait. You can sense the weariness of someone who is just trying to make an honest dollar when an elaborate, showy comment is answered with "Thanx!"

The ongoing frenzy of getting and spending is monitored by what eBay calls "feedback," by which buyers and sellers rate each other. Feedback on eBay, whether positive or negative, tends toward the hyperbolic. Euphoric praise summarizes every transaction that is not an outright disaster: "Great seller!"; "A credit to eBay!"; "Always a sweet deal!" Such panegyrics, verbal sighs of relief at not getting cheated, are the sound of low expectations being met. Deals that end badly produce the opposite rhetorical extreme. A while back I noticed one seller citing three individuals by name and hometown in each of his listings: "The following DEADBEATS may NOT BID on any more of my auctions! PERIOD!" Dissatisfied buyers are also eager to lash out, but because eBay feedback limits the number of typed characters, their complaints often sound like the muffled cries of people who have been bound and gagged: "Ripoff artst cashd chk nevr snt item!" "Itm came broke no rply emails Jerk Jerk Jerk!" "Has my $$$ 3 mnths still no itm!" There's no closure or completeness here, only the toy collector's worst nightmare: disorder and bidding sorrow.

William Carlos Williams once called for his fellow poets to retreat from abstractions and to entertain "no ideas but in things." This credo of high modernism will also appeal to someone who is trying to counter the oppressive ubiquity of ideas with the material satisfactions of vinyl and plastic. Any English professor can tell you that language is endlessly fascinating. And yet, even an English professor might occasionally feel suffocated by language: all this reading, writing, interpreting, reinterpreting, and talking about it all over again in the classroom. At such times, it matters a great deal that a playset figure is not just the representation of something—a knight, a cowboy, a soldier—but that it also *is* something: an artifact that you can hold in your hand, place on a desk, and move from here to there and back again. The physical properties of these little people and animals are inseparable from their appeal. What are they made of? How flexible are they? How does the light play off of them? These are not empty questions. When it comes to vintage playset figures, matter matters— not least as a welcome respite from words.

Of course, *these* are words, aren't they? And don't words inevitably signal a reassertion of mind and purpose? The irony is not lost on me that I'm still looking, interpreting, and writing, though for once I am not studying marks on a page. Even here, with these petroleum-based bits of matter, it is impossible to keep narratives from asserting themselves. With playset figures, as with everything else, there can be no old and new or good and bad without history, without a story. If I don't know this particular story, how will I know which figures to bid on?

So here it is. In the beginning God created the toy figure made of lead, the "tin soldier," and saw that it was good. But lead was expensive, so on the second day God—in the guise of Charles Goodyear—learned how to harden or "vulcanize" natural rubber so it could hold a shape. This was also good: preexisting molds for lead figures could now be used to make cheaper figures out of rubber. On the third day, which arrived during the Second World War, God inspired industrial chemists to create synthetic, petroleum-based vinyl in response to shortages of natural rubber. This was also good: figures in rubberized vinyl were more flexible and less prone to drying out and cracking. On the fourth day, God made his scientist minions create a variety of polyethylenes or soft plastics: these were good because their thinner consistency filled the molds more completely, thereby producing figures that registered finer detail.

This evolution in materials brought changes in look and style. The figures in rubberized vinyl, generally from the late forties and early fifties, retained the plumpness of the earlier lead figures and gave off an oily smell. These vinyl figures, usually issued without bases, were freestanding little people whom even mild warping could change into free-falling little people. Many of these older figures were later given bases to improve their stability, especially when the shift to soft plastic resulted in lighter-weight figures that toppled over at the slightest provocation.

After soft plastic made it possible to achieve finer detailing at smaller scales, playset figures underwent a reduction in size, with significant savings in the cost of materials. When Marx made this shift in the mid- to late fifties, the standard height of an upright playset human shrank from sixty millimeters to fifty-four. Everything else got downsized, too: buildings, vehicles, and other accessories. At this point, the older 45-millimeter sets, whose parts could not be mixed and matched with the newer sets, were phased out. By the early sixties, most Marx playsets existed in a 54-millimeter world; even my beloved Mineral City street front was reissued with the newer, smaller cowboys. The fact that I was outgrowing these toys just as this shrinkage was taking place explains why I'm old-school, a confirmed 60-millimeter man.

The fifth day saw the increasing use of cheaper, stiffer plastics that gave playset figures an unpleasant surface sheen. When sellers boast that their offerings have a "flat" finish, they're assuring you that these are older items, and not the "Heritage" reissues in the later, waxier plastics. If God was still paying attention, he would not have called the fifth day good—nor the sixth. On that day, the Marx company moved much of their production overseas and tried to create a second market for their older, 60-millimeter figures by recasting them in hard plastic. This is the origin of the Warriors of the World series: fighters from various old sets, factory-painted in garish colors. Another new practice was to downsize 60-millimeter sets and reissue them in this same painted hard plastic; at an inch or so tall, these figures were hard to see, let alone play with. Although the decision to move much of the manufacturing to Mexico and Hong Kong was an obvious attempt to cut labor costs, I don't understand why the company shifted to hard plastic unless it was cheaper. The factory painting was most likely a response to the demand for more colorful toys which arose with color television.

Meanwhile, child's play was starting to make its oft-lamented, TV-reinforced move from active participation to passive observation. I'm grateful that I missed the playset shift from play to display. If you're only observing, a tiny figure is as good as a larger one: all you have to do is look closer. And if the figure isn't really meant to be played with, it won't matter that it has been cast in breakable hard plastic. These later items were already being marketed as collectibles rather than real toys. This explains why the brittle, painted Warriors of the World were given names and sold in individual boxes, with little cards that narrated each figure's fictive "biography."

Although God was surely averting his eyes by now, the seventh day found Louis Marx and Company resting, too: its long run, which had begun in 1919, came to an end. Collectors and hobbyists soon took over, and a brisk business of producing recasts from old Marx molds sprouted up to meet the demand. Some of these recasts are now old enough to be called "vintage"; they are identifiable from their stiffer plastic and vivid colors, the latter a clear contrast with the white, cream, gray, and earth tones of early, original Marx figures. These new colors and materials reflect the economics of the collectibles market. If the makers of recasts were to produce copies that could not be distinguished from the originals, collectors would be outraged. Scarce items acquired over the years would, in effect, no longer be scarce—and every collection would immediately lose value.

Collectors would get even angrier at the fact that all of our hard-won expertise would suddenly be rendered useless. Within our small corner of reality, we know what the authentic stuff is; our faith in the good and the true, so often denied in the larger world, can at least be satisfied *here*, on this minor-league stage. This is the deeper reason why collectors find well-made copies so appalling: they cheapen the vintage toy as an icon of tiny but controllable perfection, controllable because it is tiny, and perfect because it is unlike everything that lies beyond our control and is therefore not perfect. Obvious fakes are fine for filling a gap or two in a collection, but realistic fakes destroy the very basis of collecting: the ideal of scarcity.

Whether we collect coins, stamps, or playset figures, collectors are constantly seeking an imagined order that just as constantly eludes us. This is due, in part, to the fact that little beacons of order come with no guarantees. I once bought a big lot of "vintage rubber figures," photographed in a see-through bag under a glare, that turned out to be cheap 1980s plastic from Hong Kong. On another occasion I discovered that a set of Auburn Rubber cowboys described as "rubber-like vinyl" were actually in the later soft plastic, which the company used after leaving Indiana to make its last stand in Deming, New Mexico. When the seller claimed to be unable to tell the difference, I gave him an insider's tip of my own: vinyl usually sinks and soft plastic usually floats.

Although I'm a stickler when it comes to materials, I am cheerfully indifferent regarding the condition of these figures. Unlike that pioneers winner, I need evidence that a toy was once loved before I can love it. An object sealed in a living tomb of cellophane, see-through plastic, or cardboard has more to do with lucre than with love, which is why broken figures are fine with me. The fact that they are usually missing their weapons also makes them more versatile as objects of midlife contemplation. A Warriors of the World Viking with his spear broken off can be reimagined as a big, gentle lug selling baskets at a Renaissance fair. Robin Hood archers with missing bows can be creative anachronists doing Tai Chi. A G.I. stripped of the rifle that he originally waved can be a ham actor chewing the scenery in *Othello*. Far from diminishing these figures, incidental damage augments their capacity for some real play.

Deliberate damage is another thing altogether. It disturbs me to confront hacked limbs, melted faces, and pinholes. I can understand how a boy who has been prematurely forced to read *Ivanhoe* might develop sufficient Anglophobia to take a pocketknife to a Sons of Liberty redcoat. But why chop off the arms of a flag-bearing colonist—one of *our* guys? Could this mayhem have been committed by a homesick young Brit, a diplomat's child convinced that he would gag if he had to eat one more hot dog? Not even plastic members of Tom Brokaw's "greatest generation" are immune from such abuse. Although I burned my share of Nazi soldiers as a child, I would never have dreamed of harming a Battleground G.I. And yet, here is a G.I. with a cleanly severed foot: did a sullen contemporary of mine amputate it to get back at his father for those endless stories about Anzio? Here is a cowboy with half a head, perhaps the self-righteous handiwork of a fledgling vegan who sought revenge on this tiny enabler of animal slaughter. Or perhaps these figures once belonged to the young Jeffrey Dahmer, and even darker impulses were at work.

At least an intentionally damaged G.I. conveys a disturbing truth that fifties playsets routinely downplayed: in war, horrible things like this actually happen. This raises the possibility of a softer interpretation: maybe our young culprit was a fatherless boy who knew this fact all too well. How could Dad get killed in Korea, when these stupid toy soldiers that Mom got me don't have a scratch on them? Regardless of what motivated the damage, I feel considerable solicitude toward these grotesques. Damaged figures are worthless as collectibles, but I'll take them anytime because they give my collecting a degree of altruism. Whatever these guys have been through, it's all behind them now.

I have gradually come to accept the fact that there are some playset figures that I will never acquire. These are the plastic and vinyl equivalents of the Holy Grail or the Ark of the Covenant, though the Ark exists in a 60-millimeter replica that an eBayer from Colorado sells for an opening bid of twenty-five dollars. When a genuinely rare figure comes up and the bids start to climb, I watch with fascination, envy, and—at least, most of the time—inaction. I have too much pride, or perhaps shame, to bid what it would take to win it. Let the crazy people fight it out; surely I'm not that kind of a collector.

Besides, why would I want to end my fantasy of a desktop populated with objects of unattainable desire, those rarest citizens of play-set Shangri-La? Sometimes I indulge this fantasy by imagining myself acquiring these unobtainable figures for free—a pleasant daydream of getting without spending that owes its genesis to Detroit Dave's dinosaur story. This daydream puts me in Glen Dale, West Virginia, where I have just located the "Marx dump," a semi-legendary site that supposedly yields plastic gold even after all these years. Armed with a shovel and a large burlap sack, I start digging. Except for the singing of Appalachian birds and the gentle lapping of the Ohio River as it flows nearby, the scene is utterly quiet.

My first shovelful turns up a thousand-dollar value: the fabled 60-millimeter Moses, gleaming white in the soil like a dinosaur's tooth. The next thrust exposes the corner of a musty box that reads "Ten Commandments Playset." Aware that this set recently sold on eBay for $433, I dust off the box and gently lower it into my sack: I'll open it at my leisure when I get home. I dig deeper and catch the glint of spears belonging to the 60-millimeter Romans. Just beneath the Romans, three specks of semitranslucent purple turn out to be the Ben Hur character figures: the emperor, the empress, and Charlton Heston himself—a $212 value, if a recent eBay sale is any indica-tion. Nearby, I spy the coveted 60-millimeter Egyptians, whose antic poses make them look as if they've spent half a century clawing their way out of a pyramid. The Glen Dale plant must have performed an elaborate, history-based triage on its trash: I've discovered the dump's "ancient world" zone.

Occasionally glancing up to make sure that I'm still alone, I keep digging until the sun sinks behind a nearby mountain and it's too dark to see. As I head back to the car, my sack bulges with plastic equiva-lents of the "wonderful things" that Howard Carter saw when light first streamed into Tutankhamen's tomb: the elusive Rat Patrol fig-ures, dirty but otherwise mint; a full set of royal family figures from the 1952 Coronation set; the fabled 60-millimeter ranch kids, recently offered on eBay for $1995; complete Little Red Schoolhouse and Wagon Train playsets; a mint set of International Geophysical Year playset Eskimos; all of the Captain Gallant Arabs in flat red-brown; all of the Untouchables figures, including a mint Al Capone and Eliot Ness; and—*mirabile dictu*—a full set of Marx Skyscraper people in flat cream, a single one of which recently fetched over $200. I am especially pleased with my last find of the day, made more by feel than by sight: the four 54-millimeter *Gunsmoke* characters, which recently sold for $812. Significantly, I do *not* imagine finding a test figure of the young Mark McCain carrying a rifle, designed for the Rifleman set but reportedly rejected because Louis Marx did not want to show a boy carrying a gun. Even daydreams have their limits—and mine cannot accommodate digging up a figure that recently sold for $4,550. Why be greedy, even in the privacy of one's mind?

As I drive north toward Wheeling and reflect on what a good day this has been, the daydream dissolves. If my glorious day at the Marx dump were real, the desktop crowd would witness a welcoming ceremony to end all welcoming ceremonies. It would *be* the end, too, because there would be nothing else to want. Genuinely rare playset figures are like all the other unmet needs that keep us looking ahead. I think of these figures in much the same way that I think of Borneo: I've never traveled there, but someday I might, and I will be dazzled by an impossibly lush landscape. The fabled Marx Moses and the presumably real Borneo, twin mysteries that await future revelation, are nudging me to accept the existence of wonderful things that I cannot verify with my senses. The world of getting and spending, stocked as it is with dull realities, needs to have some room for unrevealed things like this. Pondering their unseen beauty, even in plastic and vinyl, is like confronting the flesh-and-blood self and thinking, if only for a moment, that there might be more to us than this.

Collecting Myself

Whenever we love particular things—stamps, coins, old books—with sufficient fervor to acquire as many of them as we can, something deeply personal is going on. Bill Brown, a theorist of how material objects assert themselves in literary texts, gets it exactly right when he observes that in collecting, "what you really collect is always yourself" (*A Sense of Things* 146). Because self-scrutiny is rarely pleasant, the deeper motives and satisfactions of collecting usually go unexamined, and as a result, we collectors can be both extremely knowledgeable and stunningly clueless about what we do. Although we can talk for hours about the finer points of the objects that we love, we're hard-pressed to tell why, exactly, we love them. Often we can't explain it to ourselves

It's easy to say that we collect things simply because we love them—but since the motives for love are notoriously untraceable, there's no accounting for the things that we collect. The old saw about one man's trash and another man's treasure is nowhere truer than in the realm of collecting, where the rationale is often incomprehensible to outsiders. Why would anyone need a complete run of Archie comics, every Smurf ever made, or a Pennsylvania license plate for each year in which they've been issued? Indeed, the normal ordering of priorities seems askew. Ask a collector of Topps baseball cards to name the necessities of life, and the reply might be: food, water, shelter, and Topps baseball cards.

Unless, of course, it's Donruss baseball cards, or Fleer. A collector's love is always narrowly focused, often to a myopic degree. We cheerfully bond with like-minded lovers of the Collected Thing, but not with those who collect other things. As Richard Rubin recently observed in *AARP* magazine, collectors are usually "so single-minded in their pursuit that they can't imagine why anyone would be interested in collecting anything else" ("A Mass Appeal," March/April 2008: 56). Our Topps collector sniffs that only a philistine could get excited about Donruss cards. Ask anyone who collects Star Trek memorabilia about the sense and sensibility of Star Wars collectors, and the answer will be much the same. Our passions are far too specific and varied to result in anything like a general "collecting community."

For all the sniping between Pepsi-paraphernalia people and Coke-paraphernalia people, however, collectors have always shared some identifying traits, a family resemblance. In medieval times, those whose instincts were to hoard things were called "winners"; those who consumed things before they had a chance to pile up were called "wasters." Now that eBay has become the premier forum for collecting in America, the term "winners" has received an updated and more literal nuance. Still, the temperament persists.

The most important thing to understand about collectors is how easy it is to misread us. Our passion for material objects conceals the fact that we tend to live deeply—often excessively—in our minds. Beneath our bright certainties and buoyant enthusiasms lies a fierce rage for order, a passion for closure and completeness. We spend hours acquiring, sorting, cleaning, repairing, and arranging objects in a constant battle against chaos, randomness, and decay. At root, we are pie-in-the-sky Platos stumbling through an Aristotelian world of the senses. Obsessed with ideal forms, perfect groupings, and completed wholes, we try to fill these imagined templates with fallen objects that never quite match the mint exemplars in our minds.

Any foe of chaos will develop unusual gifts of discernment, especially an ability to read dark omens lost on outsiders. Our hearts sink as we examine a Wedgwood plate and spot a hairline crack that a normal person would dismiss as no big deal. We frown as we notice a tiny dent in one corner of the Bubble Wrap that encases a mint-on-card He-Man figure. The left knob on the drawer of this Victorian music box is a shade darker than its mate: it is clearly a replacement, and an inept one at that. Some ignorant fool has exposed this otherwise mint copy of DC Comics number 91 to direct sunlight: see how the red in Superman's cape has faded?

Our expertise grows as we collect, and before long, we know a lot of obscure things that other people don't. Our status as an expert in the Collected Thing encourages a tendency to show off. If anybody is interested in vintage playset figures, I have become a genuine go-to guy: how can I not be something of a snob about that? I can give an approximate date to a 54-millimeter Marx cowboy that has a base stamped by two small circles, a magical ability that came with learning that the company didn't start putting a logo on its figures until 1963. I can tell you—assuming that you need to know—whether a Marx dinosaur is an original or a reissue from a mere glance at its color and sheen. And do you, by any chance, own a Marx General Patton? If the figure is white and cast in hard plastic, it's an original; if the plastic is green and soft, it's a recast made in England in the 1990s. Is this useful knowledge? It certainly is to the collector, if only to avoid acquiring items that are not what they seem. Such knowledge, however, comes with a downside: its narrowness underscores an infinitude of genuinely useful things that we might have learned instead.

Within our tight little purviews, collectors get excited way too easily—and we know it. Our specialized enthusiasms have provoked too many blank stares for us not to downplay them to outsiders. This makes us obsessed people who are constantly trying, usually without success, to appear normal. Watch as a collector enters a shop specializing in the Collected Thing: his or her eyes will dart this way and that in a rapid-fire calculus of assessing, eliminating, and zeroing in. Knowing that our excitement, if noticed, will increase the price, we try to remain calm and, yes, "collected." Maintaining the proper restraint is not easy: whenever I scan new listings of old toys on eBay, my eye movements are those of a rabbit. But no "winner" likes to lose, and the competition with like-minded peers soon makes us cagey. I have a friend who, upon spotting a promising piece in an antique store, will leisurely walk around studying everything *but* the piece, sneaking only quick, sidelong glances. She has mastered the collector's first lesson: if you are seen wanting something badly enough, other people will want it, too.

Despite the competition, the little world of the Collected Thing is a gregarious place—a buoyant community of sellers and buyers, feared competitors and friendly trading partners, old hands and neophytes. Such sociability contrasts sharply with how collectors often experience the everyday world, where we are utterly alone with our enthusiasms. Such solitude lends a degree of sheepishness to our collecting:

admitting to any kind of love is hard, but it's even harder when the appeal of the beloved object eludes everyone who does not also love it. This mix of arcane knowledge and social isolation accounts for our classically adolescent aura. We try to look like perfectly presentable adults in our ordinary lives, and sometimes we succeed. In our collecting lives, however, we are big, goofy kids—like Peter Pan, but very, very earnest.

Despite this emotionally stunted, record-shop vibe, hard-core collectors tend to be older people. A 2000 marketing study, cited by Rubin, confirms that the majority of self-identified collectors are over fifty; fewer than 11 percent are under thirty-six (54). On reflection, this makes perfect sense. For one thing, younger people might be expected to be natural "wasters," living in the Aristotelian moment of whatever presents itself to their senses. For another, people in their twenties and thirties are just starting out in a more broadly conceived process of "collecting" as they acquire careers, spouses, homes, and children. With most of these big-picture needs met, we older types often shift the habit of acquisition to smaller-picture needs, to our collections.

This is not greed, exactly. By keeping acquisition alive, collecting helps keep *us* alive. The objects that we seek create a future—a temporal zone in which something very good might turn up, if only we keep looking. This sense of futurity provides a welcome antidote to the darker visions and revisions that come with getting older. Anyone who is no longer capable of running a marathon or partying until dawn will naturally develop the collector's habit of living more and more deeply in the mind. Then, too, it takes years of real-world disappointment to develop a passion for those things which will *not* disappoint: those ideal exemplars and imagined wholes. Complete settings of Depression ware, rows of Ford hubcaps hanging neatly in the garage, *Life* magazines sleeved in plastic and shelved chronologically: we cherish the order embodied in these mint objects precisely because our bedraggled selves are so disordered, so *not* mint. We know, deep down, that our collections are futile salvos against the inevitable. Years of living have taught us that all templates of order are fated to unravel—including the bundle of templates that we call the self. We gather things around us most fiercely once we can imagine our own death.

And yet, collecting is undeniably—if inexplicably—fun. According to the study that Rubin cites, thirty-seven million Americans call themselves "collectors": would so many of us keep doing something if it made us miserable? The most obvious payoff of collecting, of course, is the pure animal joy that comes with acquiring a desired object, a joy that goes back to the infant's outstretched, impatient hand. Further appeal lies in collecting's escapist dimension. To collect is to create space and time for some unlabored breaths, temporary respite from the grip of mundane duty and relentless purpose. A great irony of collecting is that we pursue this escape with relentless purpose of our own, scanning auction sites, catalogues, classifieds, and flea markets in search of the objects that move us. Make no mistake: we work at this.

It seems strange that so widespread an activity is so little understood. But as Susan Stewart and other theorists have shown, collecting is riddled with paradoxes. Foremost among them is the fact that collecting is an activity that seeks its own end. However satisfying the hunt, every collector works toward a "completed" collection—and with it, the cessation of the very process that brings so much satisfaction. This suggests an even deeper paradox: while the collector takes pleasure in owning a coveted thing, a greater pleasure lies in *not* owning it, at least not yet.

Because collecting is all about anticipation, fulfillment is both the goal and the enemy. We want to "collect them all," as those cereal boxes containing cheap trinkets and those gas station displays of tumblers of the States once urged us to do, but if we ever did, all fun would cease. There's little risk of this if the Collected Thing is still being produced, like Franklin Mint porcelain figurines or those "limited-edition" plates advertised in *Parade* magazine and the *Reader's Digest*. But when the objects in question aren't being made anymore, there exists a potential end—and therefore, a serious threat. Suppose you finally manage to collect them all, and an imagined whole becomes an actual, completed whole? What then? The easy answer, and the most common one, is that there is always something else to collect, if only duplicates and better exemplars of what we already have. The collector always has something to look forward to: is it any wonder that older people cling to the future that the hobby ensures? As the years pile up, something has to keep us from feeling overwhelmed by the daunting heft and bulk of our own pastness. Accordingly, the ultimate value of the desired item lies in the fact that it remains firmly and brightly ahead of us. Suppose that you're seeking a mint Luke Skywalker to go with the slightly playworn Princess Leia that you acquired last month. Once you get Luke, you'll want to replace your old Leia with a mint Leia. All such objects reside in an imagined "later"— and thank goodness that they do.

This anticipatory thrust masks collecting's utter impracticality. Collecting creates nothing, produces nothing, and helps no one—except, of course, collectors in their struggle against mortality. Yet, even here the comforts are limited, because no outcome is possible beyond the certain end of a completed collection or, even more certainly, of a completed life. Collectors merely reorganize preexistent objects into new but temporary configurations, clinging to these objects until we decide—or someone else decides for us—to disperse them into new configurations, into other collections.

While the customary balm for what medieval people called *timor mortis*—the fear of death—is to grab our fellow mortals and tell them who we are, collectors are denied this balm by the narrowness of our enthusiasms. This accounts for the persistent sadness of collecting: we want to display our collections, but to whom, exactly, can we display them? Despite the time, effort, and money that we've spent building up this particular assemblage, outsiders are unlikely to "get" what we've done or why it matters. What's more, our attempts to educate them only make us feel more pathetic. A captive onlooker—perhaps a dinner guest—shuffles his feet and forces a smile as we explain how hard it was to find this particular Collected Thing. It's a "good story," as we always label our good stories: a revered collector from Cleveland died, and his collection was being dispersed on eBay while I was on a business trip. Can you believe it? *I almost missed bidding on this!*

There's no escaping this sadness. Our animated tales of acquisition expose the fact that every collection is a still from a movie—a temporary stay against the uncontrollable flux of all things under the sun, including the sun. Although we may have benefitted from that death in Cleveland, it reminds us that our own collection will someday pass into other hands, perhaps those of a loathed eBay bidding rival. Even worse, our treasures may end up being unceremoniously trucked to a landfill. A constant need to shake off such thoughts accounts for the upbeat fiction that we are dispelling cosmic darkness with these little points of lights that are lining our shelves or filling our plastic bags.

When I was six or seven, frequent nightmares made me afraid to go to sleep until I finally took my mother's advice: "Just think pleasant thoughts." Mom's suggestion worked, but all too well: although the nightmares ended, the pleasant thoughts took on a life of their own. They still do. Whenever I can't sleep, it's usually not because of stressful thoughts, but because of pleasant ones and my unwillingness to shut them down. I'm living proof that sleeplessness is not always prompted by worry; sometimes it results from self-willed escapes from worry. The HealthLink USA Web site recently gave an insomnia tip that tells my story: "Nightmares and dreams that interfere with sleep may respond to psychological interventions." Although pleasant thoughts have indeed proved an effective psychological intervention, they make it impossible to say whether I have insomnia or not. Is sleeplessness insomnia if it's willed, if it stems from a stubborn refusal to let the mind go blank?

Reading in bed has always been my main source of pleasant thoughts. Recently, however, I've supplemented this ritual with a new one. Each night I choose a handful of old playset figures, set them up on my bedside table, and watch under dim light as they generate stories to grow sleepy by. My choices, however random, almost always suggest something interesting. Romans and cows, for instance, might evoke tales from a really old West; spacemen and dinosaurs, a shuttle mission back to the Mesozoic; dollhouse kids and elephants, a junior Peace Corps program in India. The fluid randomness of such vignettes stimulates new and often absurd stories that are perfect for breaking the maddening circularity of a racing mind.

To gaze at spacemen, dollhouse kids, or Roman cowboys is to employ a visual mantra that is similar, in its ritual efficacy, to more common sleep aids: chamomile tea, a leisurely bath, a glass of warm milk, the familiar glow of Leno, Letterman, or O'Brien. This last is a big one: a recent National Sleep Foundation poll revealed that 87 percent of American adults watch television as part of their pre-sleep ritual. Many experts, however, advise against this because TV can prove too stimulating. I can attest that playset figures can pose the same problem. Once you start spinning too good a story—say, a scenario in which the Marx Jungle Jim missionary is trying to convert a herd of woolly mammoths—the effect will be the same as watching a late-night movie: however cheesy the plot, you'll want to see how things turn out.

Some of these bedside vignettes have embodied stories that are not invented but remembered. I have reenacted *The Honeymooners*, starring a recast Marx Jackie Gleason—"recast" in both senses here—along with Pat Brady as Art Carney and a pair of Marx dollhouse mothers as Audrey Meadows and Joyce Randolph. With the help of Atlantic Greeks and Trojans, I have relived the pathos of Priam begging Achilles for the return of his son Hector's body. I have watched an Ideal naval officer and a Marx Captain Gallant legionnaire pointing at each other in theatrical gestures of *j'accuse* during the Dreyfus trial. And in the reenactment of an especially vivid memory, I have restaged the Kennedy-Nixon debates at 60-millimeter scale.

Bedside music also soothes the savage breast—or is it beast? My inner ear has savored the "musical stylings," as a fifties nightclub host would put it, of a four-piece combo called the Brown Cowboys, made up of the guitar-playing cowboy from Auburn's Western Roundup set, the seated guitar player from the Marx Bar-M Ranch, and two Marx "special town" cowboys, one playing a Marx dollhouse piano and the other sitting behind a plastic drum kit that came with some hideous Beatles figures from Hong Kong. The Marx Jesus and the apostles have taken the bedside stage as the First-Century Mediterranean Glee Club, their repertoire consisting not of hymns—that would be too predictable—but barbershop chestnuts like "Down by the Old Mill Stream," which was written in my Ohio hometown. Pat Brady and the Bar-M cowgirl frequently perform as a versatile vocal duo: depending on my mood, they have been Nelson Eddy and Jeanette MacDonald, Ike and Tina Turner, Porter Wagoner and Dolly Parton, and Sonny and Cher. They have not been Roy Rogers and Dale Evans, because Standing Roy and Ravishing Dale are here in the flesh—or rubberized vinyl—to sing for themselves. In more highbrow moments I have drifted off to *The Great Gate at Kiev* and the overture from *William Tell*, performed by an orchestra of medieval lutists, Roman trumpeters, Civil War buglers, Revolutionary War drummers, and cowboy guitarists. Sitting Roy plays the tympani, just as I did in high school.

The most consistent source of nighttime daydreams has been the

Troupe: some thirty figures in bedside residence whose talents encompass every possible showbiz diversion. With the Brown Cowboys serving as house band, the Troupe contains singers (Sitting Roy, Ravishing Dale, a Captain Gallant legionnaire), stand-up comics (Pie Man from the Marx Fairy Tales set, along with Pat Brady and the Bar-M cowgirl when they're not harmonizing), actors (the Jecsan Roman senator and matron and the Auburn Noah and his wife, here named Nick and Nora Noah), a magician (an Atlantic Egyptian whom I've dubbed Imhotep, after the legendary architect of the Step Pyramid), and a pair of Marx bathing beauties who act, sing, dance, and perform an excellent smart-girl/dumb-girl comedy routine. There is a master of ceremonies (the Marx 3-inch construction foreman) and a writing staff (the Marx Skyscraper boss, the 60-millimeter Friar Tuck, and the 60-millimeter Maid Marian). Two well-heeled patrons keep everything afloat: Marx dollhouse parents whose Troupe names are Gordon and Katherine Dalhousie. The smiling Friar Tuck doubles as Troupe therapist, Pie Man doubles as caterer, and a vinyl Marx MP handles security. There is also a permanently seated audience whose enthusiasm is clear from their gestures of approval: the Auburn cowboy who hoists a cup of coffee; the Marx Western Town cowboy who grins and waves; and Sitting Roy, who watches the acts whenever he's not performing.

The Troupe offers an ongoing blend of Chautauqua, Interlochen, and the Catskills—and there's never a dull moment. Each night its members entertain each other, and me, with something different: scenes from *Oedipus Rex* or *King Lear*, dance routines, lectures and speeches, concerts, or an endless variety of vocal performances. Sometimes the Troupe performs for a rotating audience of visiting figures. In time-bending USO tours, they have entertained Roman gladiators, medieval knights, and French Foreign Legionnaires. They have given benefit performances for the combined wounded of the Civil War and WWII and staged post-armistice spectaculars for American, German, and Japanese soldiers. They have performed for U.S. presidents, Cleopatra, and Davy Crockett in two sizes—a frontier father and son. They have even taken on the ultimate playset-figure challenge: command performances for Louis Marx himself.

Occasionally, the Troupe relaxes by serving as an audience for other figures. They have witnessed rodeo acts, medieval jousts, and close-order marching drills performed by the Training Center honor guard. They have heard the Gettysburg Address delivered in stereo by two Lincolns in two sizes. They have been blessed by the Reamsa Medieval Court monk and by the two Marx Jesuses, with both hands. They have marveled at death-defying leaps by the Marx Super Circus acrobats and roared at the slapstick of the Super Circus clowns. They have seen Marx dinosaurs square-dancing and western horses prancing in formation like the Lipizzaners. The gamut of entertainment, from low to high, has unfolded before their eyes: from a night at the Folies-Bergère, courtesy of the Marx bathing beauties, to a somber Christmas pageant featuring the Marx Nativity figures and a supporting cast of apostles.

As the bedside Christmas pageant suggests, play is never just fun and games. On the night when my mother called at two in the morning to tell me that my father had died in his sleep, there was nothing to do but try to get some sleep of my own before leaving for Ohio the next day. After tossing and turning for a couple of hours, I suddenly realized that something was missing. Although Dad's death had been quick and painless, there had been no proper deathbed scene like in the movies: no gathered family leaning in for final blessings calmly conferred by a dying patriarch. As Mom described it, there was only a non-story: two unusually deep breaths followed by utter stillness. Playset figures have been convincing me, however, that bad stories and non-stories can be rewritten into better ones, provided that the appropriate personnel are at hand. And so they were—or rather, so *we* were. I finally drifted off by gazing at a scene of deathbed closure that should have happened but, failing that, was happening here and now. As with all rituals, arranging this vignette prompted a comforting shift from stasis to movement. As I put the Auburn Rubber lineman in a Marx dollhouse bed and placed our family stand-ins around him, helplessness gave way to a feeling of agency vital not just to grieving, but to the human condition generally.

In the 1930s, historian Johan Huizinga described our species as *Homo ludens*, the "playing human." The theory that human consciousness was formed from play makes a lot of sense: we became people once we moved from utilitarian acts of survival to seemingly gratuitous exertions with no apparent adaptive value, except perhaps as counters to boredom and fear. There was a time when living in a cave was a natural, practical choice. At a certain point, however, we started decorating its walls—and the rest, as they say, was history. Is it too much to claim similar value for all such retreats from sheer utility, including a retreat into collecting vintage toys? Ultimately, we play such games, in Emily Dickinson's phrase, "to keep the dark away"—or more bluntly, because we're all going to die and there's nothing we can do about it. We can lament our cosmic victimhood and howl like a bunch of Marx dollhouse babies, or we can pick things up and move them around a bit, arranging and rearranging what we can in an attempt to ease whatever hurts us. And because we possess consciousness of our own deaths, something is always hurting us.

Play thus stands in close relation to humor and its undercurrent of pain. The French philosopher Henri Bergson defined comedy as an unexpected juxtaposition of rigidity and fluidity: our relentless rage for order being ambushed by the chaos of real life. The prototype of all comedy is the pompous man—rigidity personified—who slips on a banana peel. When he ends up seeing stars, we laugh despite the knowledge—or more likely, because of it—that someday *we'll* be seeing stars.

Several weeks later, just before my father's memorial service, I set up a second vignette. I knew that this would be a Unitarian service, with no talk of heaven. I no longer believe in heaven—at least, not in the way that my grandmother once described it to me. Still, old stories die hard. Was it mere superstition to conjure my handsome American Dream father in the guise of the Auburn Rubber lineman and place him beside a Marx Jesus to receive the Troupe's ovation for a life well lived? Was I hedging my bets regarding the Christianity of my childhood, or was this simply a tangible thing to do—a private ritual that helped me imagine my father young and strong again? I honestly don't know. Nor do I know whether it is enough to say that in the end my motives didn't really matter. I only know that enacting this bedside celebration of my father's life brought a measure of comfort. The Greek word for resurrection is *anastasis*: literally, a "standing up." When I took that Auburn lineman and stood him up, it felt as if I were re-embodying my father, coaxing him back into material existence.

If you own an antique Hallicrafters radio, you'll find yourself trolling for old tubes and other parts in order to keep the thing running. Provided that you don't also own fifteen other Hallicrafters radios, this is not true collecting: it's too rational for that. True collecting consists of acquiring objects that we *do not need*. This is why the specific connection between the lived life and the Collected Thing often seems tenuous and even antithetical. And yet the connection is always there, provided that we look closely enough. The gentle soul who collects old firearms might be collecting himself by collecting precisely what he is not. The same holds for the devotee of the local farm market who collects everything having to do with Elsie, Borden's mass-advertising cow. These people are collectors in an ironic mode, shoring up the self by indulging its flipside.

When a teacher of older literature, like Milton and the Bible, finds himself amassing hundreds of dirty little secrets in rubberized vinyl and soft plastic, questions of motive cannot be evaded. An English professor's expected commitment to the life of the mind has seemingly gone out the window; what's more, the biblical command against the worship of "graven images" sounds like divine disapproval of a highly absorbing hobby. Milton, who would naturally side with the Bible, might wonder—as I've been wondering—why a middle-aged academic, whose passion for material objects has always been limited to books, would become so enamored with vintage playset figures. Why not signed first editions, authors' manuscripts, or ceramic busts of Dickens? Why not antique maps of London or the Lake District, or T-shirts that say things like "I [heart] *The Faerie Queene*"? If Bill Brown is right, what about myself have I been collecting?

Two answers have emerged, neither of them definitive. The first is that I am an ironic collector, perhaps even to the point of self-renunciation: a bookish person who collects playset figures precisely because they have nothing to do with books. But collectors can never escape themselves, not really. An English professor—someone who writes and talks about stories—will eventually discover that toy people and animals feed this impulse by demanding fresh narratives to encompass them. This truth dawned on me only gradually, as I compulsively arranged my acquisitions into endlessly changing combinations of disparate figures. When you place a Marx G.I. beside an Auburn cowboy, you cannot avoid devising a story in which the two might interact.

A second motive seems more obvious: perhaps I've been succumbing to the tug of nostalgia after all, collecting old playset figures as a way to re-collect my boyhood. This answer rings true, but only to a point. Some of these figures have evoked powerful childhood memories, but I have been feeling a stronger—and opposing—impulse to bring them into current experience, to connect them with who I am today. This explains why I've been attracted to the figures, but not to the playsets with which they came. Time and circumstance have turned all these little people and animals into "loose" figures, to use a collector's term. Blissfully detached from the old narratives with which I grew up, they have underscored how distant and stale those narratives have become. I suspect that this desktop crowd has been urging me, all along, to rewrite a middle-aged sense of loss into a brighter story that might take me forward. To learn to play again—to let old things go and to free things up a little—is not a bad midlife lesson, not least because it allows me to justify my love for the little objects that have been teaching it to me.

Although self-justifying narratives are always suspect, telling them is precisely what we collectors do. If you're a collector, you understand. If you aren't, you might still be wondering why anyone would collect old playset figures. While I can't speak for anyone else, I have finally found an answer that feels right for me. These figures have facilitated some midlife self-medicating of a decidedly homeopathic nature: "like cures like," or, in this case, nostalgia cures nostalgia. I needed to revisit my fifties beginnings in order to get more comfortable with endings—and with moving forward despite their inevitability.

Once I understood what these old toys were telling me, a spell was broken. After nearly four years and over a thousand playset figures, my collecting mania has begun to subside. These old toys pulled me in at middle age, but they are also setting me free by doing exactly what they did when I played with some of them as a child. The sense of renewed action that they've sparked has allowed me to make sense of my collecting life and, by so doing, to move beyond it. In short, I think I've finally collected myself.

It feels right to end this extended reverie on old toys where it began, with the 60-millimeter crowd that stands before me. My father is here as the Auburn Rubber lineman, and so am I, as Simon the Zealot. How could we not both be present, given the indistinct line between the dead and the living that exists within this crowd of embodied memories? While there's no escaping the absurdity of a middle-aged man gazing at a bunch of old toys and feeling both shored up and unaccountably sad, it sure beats howling like a doll-house baby. At the very least, these figures have generated rituals that have provided a sense of control, however illusory, over the inevitable. Ritual actions have always helped us embrace the unstoppable fluidity of time—what Bergson might call the Big Joke—before time reduces us to rigidity. Ritual objects have always eased our sense of insolidity by making us feel in touch with something more solid than we know ourselves to be. I move playset figures from here to there as a small exertion of agency before it's my turn to be moved from here to there.

Like all collections, mine will never be completed. The old claim that Marx playsets came "complete in the box" was never really true, because completeness exists only in the mind as a temporary pause in our ever-shifting desires. Even this particular desire—my obsession with playset figures—has shifted. Although there are plenty of gaps in my collection, I have developed a bidding reticence that would have been unimaginable a few short months ago. The thought of buying five additional Captain Gallant Arabs just to get the standing rifleman is not nearly as attractive as it once was. I have finally made peace with the fact that I will never own a 60-millimeter Marx Moses or the fabled Roy Rogers ranch kids. And what if I did? Don't we always want more?

My collecting days are winding down, but the play will go on. I know this because the blessed rage for order, as Wallace Stevens called it, is sometimes a rage for disorder—an uncontrollable impulse to break out of old, worn-out frames. I am grateful to these lumps of vintage vinyl and plastic for freeing things up. And who's to say that they won't continue to serve as writer's little helpers, their arrangements and rearrangements serving as catalysts for some fresh narrative thinking? If I put any two or three of these figures together and ask "What's the story here?" the result will always be something new, something that will jar me out of this or that mental rut.

The little world on my desktop might even help me resume my big-world role as a literature professor. The time seems right to get back to that project on the Gospel of Mark; for reasons I don't entirely understand, I feel ready to take it up again. While it would be nice to be urged on in this work by a 60-millimeter English professor, Simon the Zealot will provide ample moral support. I'll probably summon the rest of the apostles and the Marx Jesus as additional cheerleaders, just as I did when I last taught the New Testament course. Flesh-and-blood literary historians need all the help we can get, even if it's imaginary. Scholarly writing is lonely work, performed in what often feels like a vacuum. I know that there will be days when key arguments will fall apart and the whole enterprise will seem reductive, naïve, or just plain wrongheaded. On such days I'll be counting on Jesus and the apostles to encourage me, in their Aramaic-accented English, to keep plugging away because—as they would surely put it—the night is coming, when no literary historian can work.

Standing Roy and Ravishing Dale, less informed about the New Testament but just as eager to help, will add their voices to the chorus. So will Quizzical Al and the rest of this crowd. These figures will counter a literary historian's descent into the past by asserting a bold present in rubberized vinyl and soft plastic. If I wander too far into empty abstractions, their stubborn materiality will keep me grounded. While I work, they will play—and in the process remind me that work can become so absorbing that it can feel like play. And if I ever find myself so locked into mental rigidities that I cannot find the next step forward, I will turn to a desktop crowd whose cheerful purposelessness might get my thoughts moving again.

I know that this kind of support is a lot to ask for, but these little people and animals owe it to me. Haven't I rescued Roy, Dale, and the others from the landfill, providing them with temporary shelter in a realm that shows no mercy toward ephemeral things? Given the half-century that I've managed to survive since first laying eyes on the leading citizens of Mineral City, I think turnabout is fair play.

sightline books . . . .

The Iowa Series in Literary Nonfiction